Are Athletes Good Role Models?

Other books in the At Issue series:

Are Athletes Good Role Models?

Geoff Griffin, *Book Editor*

Bruce Glassman, *Vice President*
Bonnie Szumski, *Publisher*
Helen Cothran, *Managing Editor*

GREENHAVEN PRESS
An imprint of Thomson Gale, a part of The Thomson Corporation

Detroit • New York • San Francisco • San Diego • New Haven, Conn.
Waterville, Maine • London • Munich

GV 697 .A1 A59 2005

Are athletes good role models?

LIBRARY OF CONGRESS CATALOGING-IN-PUBLICATION DATA

Are athletes good role models? / Geoff Griffin, book editor.
    p. cm. — (At issue)
Includes bibliographical references and index.
ISBN 0-7377-2695-4 (lib. : alk. paper) — ISBN 0-7377-2696-2 (pbk. : alk. paper)
    1. Athletes. 2. Athletes—Conduct of life. 3. Role models. I. Griffin, Geoff. II. At issue (San Diego, Calif.)
GV697.A1A59 2005
796'.092'2—dc22   2004054289

Printed in the United States of America

Contents

Introduction

The children and teens of the twenty-first century are wiser and more skeptical about viewing athletes as role models than previous generations. They might respect the talent of a sports star or even want to emulate certain characteristics that helped an athlete achieve success, but they are less likely than their parents or grandparents to view their favorite players as role models off the field. Today's youth view sports stars as exciting and glamorous people, but they have low expectations of them beyond their athletic performance.

In the summer of 2002 *Washington Times* reporter Thom Loverro visited a basketball camp shortly after National Basketball Association (NBA) star Allen Iverson was charged with serious criminal offenses. Loverro noticed that many young players at the camp were wearing Iverson jerseys. Loverro asked one of the boys, "Don't you think you are glorifying his lifestyle by wearing his jersey?" He was surprised when the boy replied, "It's just a jersey, man, and he's just a basketball player." For this young fan and many others of his generation, an athlete is just an athlete—nothing more, nothing less.

One year later, during the summer of 2003, NBA star Kobe Bryant was charged with raping a young woman. Just weeks after his indictment, Bryant was named "Favorite Male Athlete" in the Teen Choice Awards, receiving 12.5 million Internet votes. Although many of those votes may have come before Bryant was charged with rape, when he showed up at the awards ceremony he received more applause from the mostly teen crowd than any other winner. The case against Bryant was later dismissed, but the fact that so many teens gave high honors to a rape suspect indicates their willingness to set aside issues of character in choosing their favorite athlete.

The way young people in the twenty-first century view athletes is a marked departure from previous generations' unconditional admiration for their sports heroes. In the past, people expected athletes to have characters to match their superlative athletic ability and were shocked when any of them had moral failings. In 1919 the news broke that the Chicago White Sox had thrown the World Series by agreeing to lose games in exchange for accepting money from gamblers. When one of the accused "Black Sox," Joe Jackson, walked out of the courthouse, legend has it that a heartbroken boy who idolized Jackson looked up at the Sox slugger and pleaded, "Say it ain't so, Joe."

One reason previous generations were more likely to view athletes as role models is that the media presented them that way. The off-the-field antics and personal foibles of sports stars were hidden from the public by a complicit press. Therefore, generations of fans did not know that Babe Ruth and Mickey Mantle, two of the biggest sports stars of the twentieth century, abused alcohol and had marital problems. Instead, fans were presented with glowing portraits of their role models that suggested the players were every bit as good off the field as they were on it.

In recent years the media has expanded dramatically beyond print and radio to include the Internet and twenty-four-hour-a-day cable news outlets giving fans access to an unrelenting flood of information about all aspects of the personal lives of athletes. The rules regarding what can be told about a player's private life have also loosened. The reporters who were once willing to turn a blind eye to a player's personal problems now see those same difficulties as a scoop. A young person cannot open the sports section of a newspaper without reading about an athlete breaking the law or going into rehab and cannot turn on the television without seeing a video clip of an athlete misbehaving or saying something foolish. Athletes are therefore less likely to be seen as role models today because young fans know so much more about them than before.

Having grown up in an age saturated with advertising, young sports fans today are likely to view athletes as mere product endorsers rather than as role models. Today's sports stars are often just as interested in having kids and teens buy the products they endorse as they are in having those same youngsters cheer for them during a game. Athletes have always been used to help sell products, but athlete endorsements seemed to reach a new level in the 1980s, when Michael Jordan became a spokesman for a wide variety of products, had a very expensive shoe named after him, and appeared in his own movie. The situation has evolved to the point where children and teens may more readily identify a sports star with the products he or she endorses than with that athlete's team.

Another factor in the decline of athletes as role models is

that many athletes do not consider themselves to be role models anymore. Most well-known professional athletes are multi-millionaires who have little contact—and little in common—with those who would turn them into role models. Many of them even state outright that they should not be, or do not want to be, role models. One of the most famous athletes to reject being a role model is former NBA basketball player Charles Barkley, who declared in a Nike commercial, "I am not a role model." Barkley may have simply been making an excuse for his own failings in this area, but he has also stated he believes that parents are the best role models for their children.

In fact, many young people are looking to adults with whom they have regular contact to be their role models. In an annual survey by the Horatio Alger Foundation, when teenagers are asked to name their role models, athletes usually finish far down the list behind parents, friends, and teachers.

The events of September 11, 2001, also affected young people's views of who they see as role models. In an article published in the *St. Petersburg Times* shortly after the tragedy, fourteen-year-old Amy Rundio stated, "My expectations for a role model have really changed. They (role models) don't have to be famous anymore, but they have to react well under pressure and do a lot for our country." Sixteen-year-old Joshua Gregg said his view of role models had changed and noted, "I find it interesting that athletes are paid millions of dollars to play a game that the average person plays for fun; meanwhile firefighters are paid so little to save lives."

The youth of the twenty-first century are looking for people besides athletes to be their role models. Some think this is a positive step for society, while others counter that there are still positive lessons that can be learned from athletes and sports.

1

"I Am Not a Role Model"

Charles Barkley

Charles Barkley was named the Most Valuable Player of the National Basketball Association (NBA) in 1993. He was also named one of the fifty greatest NBA players of all time. Since retiring as a basketball player he has worked as a television commentator.

Parents should not expect athletes to be role models for their children. Athletes are not effective role models because the children who idolize them do not have regular one-on-one contact with them. Children have a perception of the athlete created by the media, but do not know what the athlete is really like. The idolization of athletes has created a problem in the black community because children, particularly boys, grow up thinking they will make a living as professional athletes when in fact only a tiny percentage of them will ever make it to that level. It would be better if their role models were their parents and other responsible people in the community.

Nike didn't come to me with the idea to do a commercial about role models—I went to Nike with that idea. I talked to my friend the Nike executive Howard White about it, called him after thinking about it for a while, and said, "Howard, people have this role model thing completely screwed up. Is a role model just a celebrity that parents turn their kids over to? Damn, can't we do better than that? Is the best we can do for kids pointing them to celebrities they have no real chance of ever knowing?" I just thought we as a society need to do better in that area. So I asked, and Nike said, cool. And I thought it turned out great.

Remember, the main theme was "I am not a role model."

And for that, I got ripped. I'd been criticized before, of course, for having my own take on social issues. But the first time I got hit really hard was for taking that stance. There were some columnists who defended me, but mostly I got killed. I'm okay with it, though, because nobody in all this time has been able to convince me that it's wrong to tell kids to listen to their parents and not a basketball player they've never met. How crazy is it to get slammed for saying, "Listen to your parents, listen to your teachers, listen to the responsible adults in your neighborhood or people who have done something with their lives." I know it's hard to get an entire message across in less than a minute. But I still believe the message was clear enough that I thought kids need to be able to look up to folks right there around them who can teach them hard work and right from wrong.

> *How can you make somebody your role model when you don't know the person?*

Celebrities can't teach 'em that from television. People are crazy. Or maybe they're just lazy, they don't want to do the hard work, and it's easier to just turn their kids over to somebody 'cause he's famous. How stupid is that? How can you make somebody your role model when you don't know the person? All they've got most of the time is a perception of somebody off in the distance that might be totally distorted . . . or it could be the person is just misunderstood. One thing I hate is that all the general public knows about an athlete or a celebrity is what they know from the media, which is often inaccurate or incomplete. I know cases where a guy is labeled a bad guy and he's really a good guy, maybe worthy of being a role model for kids he's close to. And I know of way too many instances where the guy comes off as a good guy in the media and he's not a good guy at all. And that's a huge problem. Either way, how could that person be a legitimate role model for a kid? Because he's famous? Because he's on TV? Can he help get questions answered for you or do anything that's specific to what you need?

Television is entertainment. I love television. And in this second stage of my life it pays me well. But television is entertainment, television is celebrity. And with so few people to emulate in their neighborhoods, black kids started fantasizing about being athletes. And having dreams is great, but how can somebody on TV help give you any direction? That's a one-way relationship. A ballplayer you can only see on TV may inspire you to do great things in athletics, sure. You can look at sports all day and want to try and do things on a court or a field like that player. But that can't help you with your homework, or with real aspirations, or help you if you're having problems at home. How does an athlete help you if you're a terrible athlete but a decent student and you need encouragement to compete academically?

A Role Model Is Someone You Know

A role model should be among the people who can influence your direction in a real-life way. The best scenario is if they can be actually in your life. My mother and grandmother were my two biggest role models; my dad wasn't there. It was my mother and grandmother. A role model, in my way of thinking, is somebody who can help shape your life and what you believe in. And it can't be somebody on television, somebody you can't touch or go to for advice, or cuss you out when it's necessary or sit and listen to you. It may be more important to have mentors than role models anyway, maybe somebody you can talk to about stuff you may not feel comfortable talking to your parents about. It needs to be somebody who's not going to tell you exactly what you want to hear all the time.

> *On the whole I don't think athletics are good for black kids.*

At the time, I felt I needed to attack the subject because on the whole I don't think athletics are good for black kids. I really don't. I got to this point because every single time I go and talk to black children or teenagers at a school or at an event, they only want to play sports. I'll ask them what they want to do after high school or about their plans in the next few years and it's always "I want to play pro basketball" or "I want to play in the NFL." Every single one, it seems to me, wants to play sports for a living. It's like there's some mental block, or they've been conditioned or brainwashed to feel they can't do anything but play sports. And it's scary to me. It bothers me. Obviously, I'm not against sports; I'm thankful for everything a career in professional sports has given me. But I don't know of any other culture where the children all want to do the same thing. I've never heard of any other situation like that.

> ***All I was saying was your parents and your teachers, people you ought to be listening to, need to be your role models.*"**

I know this is complex and there are some real contradictions here because the most really influential group of black people in America is made up of a lot of athletes. There aren't any Martin Luther Kings or Malcolm Xs or Medgar Everses leading the black community right now. Almost everybody, among the most prominent people in our communities right now, who has achieved any status the past twenty-five years has done so through athletics, which in a way is really a shame. We have a lot of hardworking people, folks doing backbreaking work. But we still don't see the doctors and lawyers and engineers we need to see and need to have portrayed and need to treat as role models. And the ones we do have don't have any real platform. They're not doing anything controversial enough or scandalous enough to get profiles in the mainstream magazines. Athletes and entertainers are the only ones among us who have the platform, mostly because they're on television every day.

So when you seriously start to think about it, our kids are so limited in the number of successful black people they can see or be exposed to. They see athletes and entertainers and what else? How often do they see scientists and engineers and writers? They don't. I know in my own neighborhood, I didn't know any black doctors or lawyers or professional black folks. They weren't in the projects where I grew up. I know a whole lot of these kids I'm talking to come from neighborhoods that ain't all that different from mine.

I'm not saying that poor white kids and Hispanic kids don't

have similar issues with this, because I suspect they do, too. And I'm not saying that only professional people can be role models. A guy working the nine-to-five cleaning the streets or running the grocery store on the corner could be a great role model. You need to see honest, hardworking people and appreciate what they're doing with their lives. And just because somebody doesn't have a college degree doesn't mean he or she can't help give some direction to a kid who can't get it anywhere else. But we also need our kids to see some professional people they can aspire to be like, and they don't see enough. Every kid can't be Michael Jordan or Will Smith, and shouldn't want to be. But this is what they see in their lives every day, because for so many of them they ain't got anything positive going on at home.

Parents Are the Best Role Models

Anyway, this had been bothering me for a while and I wanted to use my own platform to address it. And I never thought so many people would miss the bigger message. I found it interesting in the spring of 2002 that somebody came up with this TV campaign: "Parents, the anti-drug." Isn't that the same point I was making in the role model commercial? That campaign is a damn good reminder. But it's nothing different from what I was saying in the role model commercial. What's different about it? It doesn't say, "Athletes and celebrities, the anti-drug," does it? I wasn't supposed to have any ideas of my own or talk about anything serious?

All I was saying was your parents and your teachers, people you ought to be listening to, need to be your role models. Charles Barkley the basketball player should not be your role model. Yeah, I can be a role model to my daughter and to kids I have some contact with. But that's not only Charles Barkley the basketball player, that's me as a father, or a parental figure. Those kids don't see me only on TV, there's an actual relationship there, or at least some association. How many people on TV do these kids have an association with? We all know the answer is "None."

But if it took me getting slammed to get some dialogue started on this issue, then it was worth it. I'd do it again in a second.

2

Athletes Are Role Models Whether They Like It or Not

Sean Paige

Sean Paige is an adjunct scholar with the Competitive Enterprise Institute (CEI), a nonprofit public policy organization. He has served as CEI's editorial director and as a journalism fellow. Prior to joining CEI, Paige was an investigative writer and columnist at the weekly magazine Insight on the News. *His writing has appeared in the* Wall Street Journal, Weekly Standard, Washington Times, Chicago Tribune, *and other publications.*

Athletes have been regarded as role models throughout history. Even when athletes say they do not want to be role models, people continue to view them that way. Society used to idolize athletes because it had an unrealistic and incomplete view of them. It is difficult for athletes to be role models today because every aspect of their lives is scrutinized by the media. While the new generation of Americans is not as enamored with athletes as past generations, there are still fans who will cheer for their favorite athletes and view them as role models.

The economics of sports entertainment have transformed many star athletes into multimillionaire prima donnas with little in common with—or use for—even their fans.

Often waiting in line overnight, crowds—sometimes hundreds of thousands strong—would surge into the stadium at first light, jostling for their places before the big game. Oblivious to the elements—slashing rain or scorching sun—spectators spent the day wildly cheering their favored team and colors to victory or defeat, with the most dramatic contests sometimes ending in sudden death or a street riot.

But the Super Bowl or World Cup this was not. It was Constantinople, circa 500 A.D., under the Roman emperor Anastasius, and on this day the Green team came through in the clutch, British historian Edward Gibbon recounts, producing daggers and stones smuggled onto the field to murder 3,000 of the Blues. Although admittedly a bloody day for the Blues, who were to avenge this loss many times over during the reign of Justinian (a stalwart Blues backer), the slaughter represented a relatively mild afternoon at the city's colossal hippodrome, where the ferocity of the contests had been only slightly tamed by the Christian influence.

From Ancient Rome to Modern America

Imperial Rome had its gladiators, America has its gridiron greats. And just as Gibbon held up Rome's growing preoccupation with grotesque circuses as a barometer betraying a society's decay, the fall from grace of America's sports idols may be auguring something troubling about our own national soul.

Of course, Americans are not yet taking "bread and circuses"—government giveaways and sport spectaculars—to the extremes described by Gibbon in his famous *Decline and Fall of the Roman Empire.* Rather than feeding Christians to the lions, our Sunday-afternoon bloodlust more often is sated by pitting the Lions against the Saints, two National Football League teams seemingly caught in a Grail-like quest for a wild-card playoff spot.

Yet in Gibbon's account of the ancients we still can see eerie reflections of ourselves: cities staking their sense of identity and prestige on the games; public funds being plundered for ever more gaudy spectacles and grandiose stadiums; "idle multitudes" of citizens, "their minds agitated with hope and fear," devoting their lives to their beloved colors; politicians being drawn into sports rivalries and issues; and a win at any cost used to excuse every excess of increasingly lawless gladiators.

"Every law, either human or divine, was trampled under foot, and as long as the party was successful, its deluded followers appeared careless of private distress or public calamity,"

Gibbon writes. Before long the empire's "dissolute youth," taking their cues from the lawless gladiators, were caught up in the mayhem, the historian reports. And because "the laws were silent" in response, Gibbon laments, "the bonds of society relaxed."

> **"** *Into the admittedly idealized world America's sports heroes once inhabited come barbarian vandals, smashing the pedestals we put them on.* **"**

The "relaxing" of societal discipline is something with which America, too, is wrestling, and our own elite athletes, once held up as heroes personifying strength, courage, fair play and other national virtues, often seem to be surfing the wave of chaos sweeping the country. Consider some of these instant replays—boxer Mike Tyson, a convicted rapist, biting a piece off the ear of [boxing opponent] Evander Holyfield; Golden State Warriors shooting guard Latrell Sprewell choking coach P.J. Carlesimo; Baltimore Orioles second baseman Roberto Alomar spitting in an umpire's face; Chicago Bulls forward Dennis Rodman kicking a spectator in the groin; and, yes, O.J. Simpson[1] trying on the bloody glove. Who will say that in all of this we are not looking at our societal pathology writ large?

Good Citizens and Barbarians

While the vast majority of our most celebrated athletes may be good citizens and worthy of emulation, increasingly the sports pages are filled with tales of criminality, greed, drug abuse, illegitimacy, spousal abuse and sexual license, with our pampered millionaire gladiators showing an impudent disregard for their actions and images. Into the admittedly idealized world America's sports heroes once inhabited come barbarian vandals, smashing the pedestals we put them on.

From baseball's Babe Ruth evolved basketball's Charles

---

1. Simpson is a former pro football star who was tried for the murder of his ex-wife Nicole Brown Simpson and her friend Ron Goldman. The jury found Simpson not guilty in the criminal trial.

Barkley, who stirred up controversy by officially repudiating his status as role model [in a Nike commercial], suggesting that parents alone should bear that responsibility.

The sports world since has split into camps: those who ascribe to the Barkley philosophy, seeing his declaration of independence as a green light for licentiousness, and those who don't, such as former college-football star and now Republican Rep. J.C. Watts of Oklahoma, who believes that an athlete's responsibilities as a citizen should temper his or her words and actions.

While Watts agrees with Barkley's point that parents matter most as role models for their children, his own experience as an athlete and politician testifies to the profound impact sports can have on character. "I agree with Charles when he says, 'Look, Mom and Dad can't put this responsibility on me,'" Watts tells *Insight*. "But I am also a firm believer that it is much more important to be a good citizen than it is to be a good athlete.

"Because of the stature and notoriety athletes have, they also have a responsibility, as citizens, to try to use whatever influence they have for positive things," Watts explains. Instead of giving him a license to indulge his personal appetites, being a star athlete "raised my awareness about my role as a citizen," says Watts, who is thankful that he always has had mentors and coaches who stressed responsibility and good citizenship.

Interestingly, Barkley made his "I-am-not-a-role-model" pronouncement in a television advertisement for Nike, which was using his name, image and reputation to promote its athletic wear—proving that in this era of the anti-hero one even can profit from thumbing one's nose at the people who put you on a pedestal. In fact, athletes have been trading on the outlaw image to sell products and heighten their celebrity—revealing a fundamental change in the way we think of them, according to some sociologists.

Sports Values

True, sport still is highly regarded in our society, celebrating virtues we revere such as competitiveness and courage. So much so that, "even though we see behavior to the contrary, we're willing to look the other way" according to University of Nevada, Las Vegas, sports sociologist Dr. Jim Frey. "We hold athletes up as role models, but we really don't expect them to be."

"We don't expect them to be value leaders, but we're not

looking for that from them," Frey says of modern sports heroes. "We're really just valuing them for their skill. Nobody knows anything about Michael Jordan's values—he's worshipped because of his skill."

"We value achievement and would like to believe that people who are so exceptional in one area are exceptional in others," adds Michael Sachs, a sports psychologist at Temple University in Philadelphia. Many professional athletes would like to take Barkley's opt-out approach on the role-model issue, says Sachs, "but most athletes recognize that in actuality they do carry that burden."

After all, most of these athletic stars have been treated as something special from the time they could hit a home run or sink a jump shot from the top of the key. "These are the elite of the elite, and they've been pampered, they've been taken care of," says Sachs, creating and reinforcing their sense that they are exceptions to the rules.

Around-the-Clock Coverage

In our celebrity-addled culture, wherein every famous person's miscues are reported by around-the-clock media, it has become increasingly difficult to find a sports figure without flaws. "In order for someone to be a hero there has to be some sense of distance between them and us" says Frey. Without that distance, "we can't keep them on a pedestal," says Frey. In the past, "the media pretty much left private lives alone; now it's no longer sacred territory."

News stories that former San Diego Padres first baseman Steve Garvey, who seemed the perfect all-American role model, had cheated on his wife and sired a child out of wedlock inaugurated the open season on sports celebrities, some sports experts say. And the hunting has been excellent ever since, thanks in no small measure to the dissolute lifestyles so many professional athletes lead in a world of fame, riches and constant travel.

Revelations concerning baseball great Pete Rose's gambling habits delivered another shock to the sports world. Then basketball legend Magic Johnson announced that he had acquired the AIDS virus, heavyweight boxing champion Tyson went to prison, figure skater Tonya Harding took out a contract on rival Nancy Kerrigan and O.J. Simpson took the nation on that low-speed chase.

Today few sports idols escape from a long career with their shining armor undented. The Mark McGwires, Cal Ripkens, Grant Hills, Emmett Smiths and Barry Sanderses are out there, of course, but their steady good citizenship often is overshadowed by ugly headlines about less-virtuous colleagues. As the venerable Green Bay Packers defensive lineman Reggie White discovered, when he ran afoul of the thought police by using complementary stereotypes during public remarks about race, even a model citizen-athlete can be just one slip of the tongue away from ignominy.

> *Sport still is highly regarded in our society, celebrating virtues we revere such as competitiveness and courage.*

Meanwhile, in this gilded age of the anti-hero many seem to delight in puncturing the inflated reputations of past heroes. Thus, Ruth was a gluttonous, drunken womanizer, we now hear, and Ty Cobb an abject scoundrel.

It may be human nature to idealize as heroes sports figures from the past, but there is little evidence that there is less sportsmanship today than there was in some supposed golden age. "My sense is that, yes, there's some poor sportsmanship out there, but I would never say that it's worse today than it was 40 years ago," says Jay Coakley, a sports sociologist at the University of Colorado at Colorado Springs. "Babe Ruth was a hayseed, but that's not the way we want to remember him. We don't want to remember him coming to the ballpark hung over after he'd spent the night with another woman; we want to remember him pointing to the centerfield bleachers" to announce a homer for a sick kid.

We remember our sports heroes—all our heroes, in fact—for their virtues, says Coakley. "To keep some sense of sanity and an anchor in our lives, we remember some things better than others."

High Pay, Low Turnout

Even as the economics of sports entertainment have transformed many of our star athletes into multimillionaire prima donnas who have little in common with the average American, those same economics may have begun to shut out and alienate lower- and middle-class fans upon whom the whole pyramid rests. "A lot of people are losing interest in [big-league sports] because they don't feel connected to it like they did in the past," explains Frey. And it's little wonder, when tickets are so expensive, the players so petulant, owners hold the fans hostage to win public financing for their stadiums and free agency has turned the roster of every ball club into a bus transfer for a list of passengers making brief stops between coaches on the road to the big bucks. . . .

Ironically, cold, cruel capitalism may be what is hurting big-league sports, which until relatively recently—when players became free agents, able to sell their services to the highest bidder—were government-assured monopolies in practice. "Leagues have traditionally been run in a socialist fashion, controlled by a cabal of owners who determined the rules of the game," protected from laws against oligopolous collusion by an antitrust exemption, explains Rick Burton, who teaches sports marketing at the University of Oregon's Warsaw Center, part of the Lundquist College of Business.

> *Today few sports idols escape from a long career with their shining armor undented.*

Courts ruled that players are not mere laborers after former St. Louis Cardinal Curt Flood petitioned the commissioner of major league baseball in 1969 to block his trade to another major-league club, Burton recounts. Flood liked St. Louis, had established a life and business there and "didn't want to be sold like livestock" Burton says. His petition eventually was denied, but Flood's refusal to be traded "was the start of the process whereby [players] started taking control of their destiny," launching the era of free agency.

While free agency has paid off handsomely for professional athletes . . . it also has given owners a handy justification to boost ticket prices, while the fans who pay those prices frequently lose track of who's on first.

"The players aren't doing anything wrong asking for as much money as they can. It's pure capitalism," says Burton.

"But it's also driven up costs all around the game." Indeed, a fan cost index produced by Team Marketing Report indicates that the cost to take a family of four out to the ball game is $114.82—which isn't peanuts, or Cracker Jacks for that matter, but is a bargain compared to the other professional sports. For a National Basketball Association game, that same family might pay more than $214. To see some professional hockey, you're talking almost $230.

> *If sports owners and promoters don't remain in touch with the young consumers, many are likely to go the way of the leather helmet and wooden tennis racket.*

As a result of the soaring costs and ticket prices, major-league sports may have "become inefficient entertainment products, because the average person can no longer afford them," says Burton.

Others may just be disgusted. Just as not every ancient Roman embraced the games, evidence suggests that many Americans are turned off by what they see, or are finding better things to do with their time and money than live vicariously through the exploits of strangers. "We have a generation coming up that isn't as enamored of football, baseball and basketball as we were," UNLV's Frey says.

A New Landscape

The sports consumers of tomorrow are the toddlers and pre-teens of today, whose athletic options and interests are incredibly diverse. And if sports owners and promoters don't remain in touch with the young consumers, many are likely to go the way of the leather helmet and wooden tennis racket.

"The sports market has to be more astute, because the niches are being drawn more narrowly," says Burton. "Today, the most powerful person in sports is the soccer mom" he tells *Insight*, because in today's climate of fear, kids just don't go down to the field or sandlot to play anymore. They spend more of their time close to home, in the yard or driveway, playing video games, or in adult-supervised activities. Peewee football may be too violent for the tastes of some modern moms, for instance, and T-ball not egalitarian enough. Americans still love sports, "but we are on the front end of a wave of change," says Burton, that is best exemplified by so-called extreme sports: competitive skateboarding, street luge, snowboarding, mountain biking, trick biking, sky surfing, pro beach volleyball, beach hockey and in-line skating, to name just a few. Such sports even have their own cable network, ESPN2, and their own championship showcase, the X-Games.

The emergence of the professional female athlete also is a major force on the new American sports landscape, experts say. A law called Title IX, which has been interpreted to require universities to spend equally on male and female athletics, is revolutionizing collegiate sports and, by extension, women's professional sports.

While female athletes long have had a high profile in tennis, golf, figure skating, gymnastics and track and field, they now are making inroads into team sports formerly dominated by men. The NCAA women's basketball tournament has received unprecedented media coverage and there are two professional women's basketball leagues; a women's professional softball league is attracting fans in many markets; and professional women boxers are achieving name recognition among fight fans.

> *Americans still doggedly root for the home team and its heroes—which in itself says something telling about the state of our society.*

While female athletes have for the most part remained unsullied by the kinds of ugly headlines their male counterparts regularly earn (with the notable exception of skater Tonya Harding), the white-hot spotlight of media attention may turn up some blemishes.

An "end of the innocence" is coming, says Washington sports attorney and columnist Ellen Zavian, when professional female athletes will begin to receive the same level of public scrutiny as their male counterparts. "Women right now are in a perfect light," says Zavian, but "are not immune from the problems male athletes have, and we're really headed in that direction."

But female fans approach their sports heroes differently than men do, says Zavian, taking a more holistic approach. Women pick a heroine "not only because of what she did on the court," says Zavian, but "girls like to hear more about their personal sides and stories." Men, on the other hand, "just want to see the stats."

Fallen but Still Relevant

Perhaps the best news, given the fallen state of America's sports pantheon, is that "the impact of sports heroes on our people is probably overblown," says Coakley, echoing the sentiments of many sports sociologists *Insight* interviewed. While the youngsters tend to relate to sports figures "because they're some of the only adults they've ever seen having fun with what they are doing," such heroes and heroines are not likely to be the determining influence on a child's life unless that child is being raised in a moral vacuum.

"We don't get these messages directly from athletes," says Coakley. "We get them from parents, coaches and friends who use athletes to make moral and character points." The lessons children may take from their big-league idols "is not an automatic transfer" according to Coakley. "The impact of what we see in sports depends upon the context in which we're living our lives."

In spite of all this, Americans still doggedly root for the home team and its heroes—which in itself says something telling about the state of our society. "The base of the word fan is fanatic, so there's not necessarily a logical basis" to the phenomenon, says Temple University's Sachs. But Americans are "all looking for some kind of community," Frey points out. "In a world where people move around and families often fall apart, sports may be the closest thing to community some people find."

3

It Is Difficult for Athletes to Be Role Models

Gary Sailes

Gary Sailes is a sports sociologist and associate professor in the Department of Kinesiology at Indiana University in Bloomington.

There are many examples of athletes who engage in criminal activity or otherwise behave poorly even though they are paid large sums of money to do something they love. However, athletes do not act in worse ways than other members of society—they just receive more media scrutiny and their problems are made known to millions of people. Athletes are also targeted by unscrupulous people because of their money and fame. Many people have high expectations of athletes that are difficult to live up to.

Is it fair to demand that athletes serve as role models? "I am not a role model! I'm a professional basketball player. I am paid to wreak havoc on the basketball court. Parents should be role models!" Charles Barkley uttered these words in a Nike commercial that stirred controversy across the country among fans and National Basketball Association players alike. His words drew criticism from players like David Robinson of the San Antonio Spurs, who felt Barkley should step up and be accountable as a role model. He felt Barkley, as a celebrity and public figure in a highly visible sports league, was a role model whether he wanted to be or not. It was simply a matter of choice: Was he going to be a good one or a bad one? As a professional athlete, Barkley was a role model, whether he liked it or not. By contrast, Allen Iverson and Dennis Rodman, two of the NBA's so-called "bad boys," were silent, much to the delight, I am sure, of league commissioner David Stern.

In light of events in the nation's headlines, the most notable being the O.J. Simpson, Ray Lewis, and Ray Carruth murder and manslaughter cases, one has to wonder: Don't athletes get it? They make millions in their contracts, are adored by fans, and are the envy of almost every red-blooded male. Why would they do anything that would jeopardize that incredibly lucrative position in our society? The problem has gotten so seriously out of hand that the images of all athletes who participate in professional sports are in jeopardy. Hooligans, thugs, and druggies are familiar words used to describe today's professional athletes.

It doesn't stop there, however. The phenomenon extends to collegiate athletes as well. The 2000–01 University of Illinois men's basketball team, as a result of their aggressive play, was labeled by the press and some opponents as the "Bad Boys." They received complaints and comments about their "dirty" play from their last opponent, the University of Arizona, who defeated them in the Elite Eight round in the 2001 NCAA Tournament.

> *Hooligans, thugs, and druggies are familiar words used to describe today's professional athletes.*

The problems surrounding the public image of professional athletes has become so apparently serious that the commissioners of the major leagues (NBA, National Football League, National Hockey League, and Major League Baseball) and the NCAA met to establish the Citizenship Through Sports Alliance. Their focus was to demand good citizenship from its participating athletes. Stern said, "You mimic behavior, good and bad, and what you see on televised games. Athletes need to accept that they are role models!"

Cedric Dempsey, executive director of the NCAA, furthered that point by stating, "Athletes who refuse to accept their obligations as role models are blind to their responsibilities as adults." Nell Austrian, NFL president and CEO, made a final plea/point when he said, "Whether they want to be or don't want to be, players are role models and enlightened people realize that." Jim Brown, Hall of Fame running back for the Cleveland Browns, argued that "Today's athlete is an embarrassment to his community!" (He conveniently ignored the fact that he has been arrested a number of times on assault charges himself.)

A Mirror of Society

I conducted a random survey of 300 college students at Indiana University, and approximately 66% felt it is the social and moral responsibility of athletes to serve as role models to America's youth, while approximately 30% believed that sport is merely a microcosm of society and consequently mirrors American culture. It is a reflection of the worst and best of society, they felt, stating that it was unfair to hold athletes to a higher standard of social and moral accountability than we hold ourselves.

For example, in a class discussion, my students asked why NBA star Michael Jordan should have been chastised for gambling when the majority of Americans gamble on golf and at casinos. So what if he gambled hundreds of thousands of dollars? To him, that was the equivalent of a noncelebrity betting a couple of hundred dollars. Because Jordan arguably was the most famous athlete in professional sports, anything he did was fair game or gossip fodder for public consumption. The students felt that it should be an athlete's decision to serve as a role model or not. They also believed that athletes should conduct themselves as responsible professionals because they not only represent themselves when they are in public, but the team/school they play for and the league they play in.

Super Rap Sheets

The reality, though, is reflected in the following past headlines, arrests, and/or convictions of a number of members of the 2001 Super Bowl teams. New York Giants: quarterback Kerry Collins—drunk driving; defensive back Sam Garnes—felonious assault; defensive tackle Keith Hamilton—marijuana possession; defensive end Cedric Jones—public intoxication; defensive tackle Christian Peter—disturbing the peace, trespassing, urinating in public, refusing to comply with a police officer, assaulting Miss Nebraska in a bar, threatening to kill a parking lot attendant, possessing alcohol while underage, and rape. Baltimore Ravens: linebacker Cornell Brown—drunk driving and misdemeanor assault and battery; tight end Ben Coates—assault and battery; linebacker Anthony Davis—negligent driving; tight end Pedro Edison—destruction of property, obstruction of justice, and involuntary manslaughter; cornerback Chris McAlister—possession of marijuana; defensive tackle Tony Siragusa—disorderly conduct, gun charges, battery; tight end Shannon Sharpa—simple battery; defensive tackle Larry Webster—soliciting a prostitute; defensive back Rod Woodson—battery on a police officer, theft, and criminal mischief; running back Jamal Lewis—shoplifting; and linebacker and NFL and Super Bowl MVP Ray Lewis—obstruction of justice (after beating a murder rap).

> **" *The students felt that it should be an athlete's decision to serve as a role model or not.* "**

Are football players out of control? In response to the press attention paid to the Carruth and Lewis trials, NFL Commissioner Paul Tagliabue maintained adamantly that the rate of criminal activity among the league's players was lower than for males in society in general, citing statistical studies to verify his point.

I question the NFL's motives. Is the league trying to produce good citizens or protect its image? Are its athletes more prone to criminal activity because of the violent nature and culture of their sport or are they just like the rest of us—normal people who sometimes make mistakes—and are made examples of because of their status? Yet, accountability is not merely an individual matter. Don't players know or care about the fact that their every move is scrutinized by fans, their coaches, and certainly by the league they play in?

Just Like the Rest of Us

I have worked with professional athletes as a performance enhancement psychologist for more than 15 years. In the process, I have gotten to know them and their families personally. I can tell you that, aside from their unusual and gifted talent, they are usually people just like you and me. They experience the same family problems other people do, have to pay bills like we do, and basically have a home life, albeit usually a larger home than the rest of us have—a lifestyle that is similar to that of many middle-class Americans, although on a far-larger scale. Athletes come from different social and cultural backgrounds and are a reflection of those backgrounds, which are fundamentally based on family and education. Believe me when I tell you that being a professional athlete is one of the most challenging professions individuals can experience, regardless of how talented or popular they become. In fact, the more successful they become, the greater the challenges they experience.

Being in the limelight presents a specific set of pressures for professional athletes, especially those who are very well known. There are people in our society who stalk, victimize, and bait athletes for financial or professional gain. Men pick fights; women they have sex with get pregnant intentionally; and news reporters may goad them into brawls. Their wealth and star status make them prime targets. The pressure to perform exerted by their teammates, coaches, owners, and fans is unrelenting. When they go out to relax and get hassled by fans—well, you can imagine what could happen. Professional athletes have to be extra careful, are always looking over their shoulders, are distrusting, and are expected to keep their noses clean and stay out of trouble. Yet, trouble often is looking for them. One bad decision, and they are blamed for letting us down. They are accused of not being good role models.

Professional athletes are expected to personify all that is good in us, our community, our society, and what is traditionally American. This is what we expect and demand from our professional gladiators. Sports agents know this and exploit this fact as they solicit product endorsements for their clients. We, as sports consumers and fans, demand nothing less. The facts, though, too often are to the contrary.

I don't think that, because of who they are, athletes' status justifies criminal behavior or sanctions the fact that they should receive special privileges in the criminal court system. Most of us fantasize about being a professional athlete. I caution you to be careful of what you wish for. Being a role model is a tough job.

4

Athletes Inspire People to Overcome Obstacles

Pat LaFontaine

Pat LaFontaine played many seasons in the National Hockey League and is a member of the Hockey Hall of Fame.

Many athletes have overcome adversity in their lives. When they face physical ailments that could end their career, they often handle the task with courage and grace. They also show a strong work ethic in battling to get back into competitive shape. Athletes are good role models because their examples can encourage others who face major challenges in their lives.

I first heard of Mario Lemieux in 1982, at the start of my first and only season in junior hockey. He and Sylvain Turgeon were the two names that kept coming up as I ventured from the United States into Canada to play for Verdun, just five minutes from Montreal.

Mario played for Laval, and we engaged in quite a duel for the scoring title, a duel I would ultimately win. My club went on to win the championship (played at the Montreal Forum, no less) and I was named Junior Player of the Year.

Mario became the first player selected in the draft and went on to a brilliant career with the Pittsburgh Penguins. Ten years after we went head-to-head for the scoring title in juniors, we matched up again in the NHL, and Mario topped me. If all we had to consider were his achievements on the ice, I would still admire him.

But Mario succeeded because he did not let injuries drive

him out of the game and because he had the guts to conquer Hodgkin's disease. When he beat me out for that NHL scoring title, he had just returned from an absence caused by cancer. Now what kind of strength does something like that take?

Mario's abilities helped save hockey in Pittsburgh, and his business savvy saved it again. My old friend and competitor owns the Penguins, having stepped in to buy a money-losing franchise and keep it from moving to another city. Mario did not grow up in Pittsburgh, but I'd call him a hometown hero. He combines heart, brains, and dedication. He was never a fighter on the ice, but he's a warrior in life.

> *Here is a professional athlete who is to be admired for the way he performed in his sport and how he conducted himself and triumphed over ill health.*

To me, that's uplifting on every level. We set our goals and dream our dreams, but we cannot know how treacherous a path we must navigate. We never know how much strength we will need or where we will find it until we really look inside. That's what makes Mario Lemieux a Companion in Courage. Here is a professional athlete who is to be admired for the way he performed in his sport and how he conducted himself and triumphed over ill health.

A Long List of Role Models

So many fine athletes achieve similar greatness away from their particular game and leave me moved by their grace, their determination, their dignity. I'm awed by the way they marshal their inner forces and refuse to bow to pain or disease. Even though I'm sharing the stories of less well-known people with you, I do want to take a moment to acknowledge some of the great names in sports. They too are Companions in Courage. You probably already know about their struggles, but I want to salute them just the same.

I'm thinking of folks like Andres Galarraga. The Atlanta Braves missed him as he sought to recover from cancer, but he came back in 2000 with that same old smile. He swung the bat just like he had never been away, and you could see that the joy in him had never left.

I'm thinking of Ernie Irvan. Here is a man who nearly died in an auto racing accident at the Michigan Speedway in 1994 and yet returned to win again. He closed out his thirteen-year career on that very same track in 1997, winning in his final race. After spending most of his forty years around racing, Ernie really didn't want to quit. But he knew the time had come. "I have two kids and a wife that mean a lot to me. The doctors told me that if I was able to drive my daughter to school that it was going to be a very pleasurable moment," he said. "This is something that I treasure."

I tip my cap to Alberto Salazar, the fine distance runner. Eight years after a disappointing fifteenth-place finish in the marathon in the 1984 Olympics, he came back to compete again for a place on the 1992 U.S. team. He changed his running style and his personal style, welcoming God and spirituality into his life while chasing out bitterness and frustration.

> *We don't win our wars without a struggle, and we don't always emerge unscathed.*

Maybe you don't know about Kevin Glover, the longtime center for the Detroit Lions and Seattle Seahawks. Back surgery could have ended his career, but he saved it by dedicating himself to, of all things, swimming. Fifteen NFL seasons, more than two hundred games, three trips to the Pro Bowl. And yet his teammates found more to respect in the bravery and intensity of Kevin Glover's efforts to return. All they had to do was watch him walk. "It's incredible that he's come back from that kind of injury," said Seahawks guard Pete Kendall. "You look at the scar and you just shake your head."

Physical and Emotional Comebacks

Scars? Monica Seles bears scars. As if defeating an opponent on the tennis court doesn't take enough concentration and energy, she had to overcome the stab wounds inflicted during a match by a knife-wielding "fan." Imagine the courage it took just to get back on the court. Flesh wounds close. Psychic wounds often require a greater strength, and I'm a Monica Seles fan because of her inner toughness. Same for Jennifer Capriati, who lost her way but managed to deal with her personal problems and make it back to the tennis tour. I'm also very moved by the plight of Chinese gymnast Sang Lan, paralyzed below the middle of her chest at the age of seventeen in 1998 after a fall during warmups for the Goodwill Games in New York. The attending physician, Dr. Vincent Leone, had himself been a high school gymnast. In comforting his young patient, he mentioned he had injured his back in his pursuit of excelling in the sport and decided to become a doctor. She told him, "Then I'll be a doctor too."

> *Isn't it just a little easier when we know that others have preceded us and we can profit by their example?*

I could go on forever. Lance Armstrong beat testicular cancer, then defeated the best cyclists in the world to win the Tour de France—[six times]. He observed, "If I never had cancer, I never would have won the Tour de France. I wouldn't want to go through that again. But I wouldn't change what happened to me." Lance emerged stronger and showed us all that a killer disease can be turned inside out. Scott Hamilton also survived testicular cancer. The gold medal winner in figure skating at the 1984 Olympics, he now runs a program called CARES (Cancer Alliance for Research, Education and Survivorship). "My dream in my lifetime is that cancer no longer exists," he said.

I remember Houston Astros manager Larry Dierker suffering a seizure on the field in 1999. I had my TV on and watched in disbelief as his athletic body flailed uncontrollably in front of a shocked, silent crowd of 39,773. It took twenty minutes to bring him under control. Finally he lay quietly enough to be strapped onto a stretcher and rolled into a waiting ambulance. The crowd and Larry's players watched as he was taken from the field. He had a blood clot in his brain. Surgeons did their job well, and Larry Dierker returned to do his well too—in a month. "Having received so many cards and letters, knowing that people all over the world were praying for me, making donations in my name to charities, such a massive show of support made me realize how important what we do is to others," he observed. "I have a new appreciation for the precious things in life. This is the most important thing that has ever happened to me in life. I am blessed."

Lessons We All Can Learn

Aren't we all, even if at times it seems we are cursed? We don't win our wars without a struggle, and we don't always emerge unscathed. But we're here, alive, in this world, and we need to take all the good we can from that, even as we prepare to give back.

Sean Elliott. Here's a basketball player who needed a kidney transplant and returned to play in the NBA. And Roger Neilson, coach of the Philadelphia Flyers, who refuses to let cancer keep him from trying to get back behind the bench. Paul Stewart, a tough American in love with hockey, who made it both as a player and an NHL referee while defeating cancer. Cris Carter, whose NFL career nearly ended because of drugs, and whose spirituality and rebirth enabled him to ultimately become one of the finest receivers to ever wear an NFL uniform.

Few lives unwind untouched by difficulties and pain. We must face and fight what fate puts in our path if we're to get to the place we want to be. Isn't it just a little easier when we know that others have preceded us and we can profit by their example?

5

Baseball Heroes Offer Lessons in Determination and Persistence

George F. Will

George F. Will is a Pulitzer Prize winner whose column appears in hundreds of newspapers weekly. He is the author of many books, including Bunts. *He also works as a television commentator.*

As the American national pastime, baseball plays an important role in society that goes beyond mere recreation. It offers lessons in excellence. In reaching the peak of their profession, baseball players must develop many positive qualities. They must work hard, pay attention to detail, constantly seek to improve, and use their intelligence. Baseball players are good examples of the work ethic that is required to become successful in any field. American society would be better off if many workers followed the example of successful baseball players.

There is, of course, a sense in which sport is the toy department of life. But professional sport, and especially baseball, has serious resonances in society. A nation's preferred forms of recreation are not of trivial importance. They are tone-setting facets of the nation's life. Scores of millions of Americans spend billions of hours a year watching baseball, listening to broadcasts of it, talking and reading and thinking about it. This pleasurable preoccupation is, at its best, an appreciation of grace, self-control and the steady application of an elegant craft.

"Knowin' all about baseball," said humorist Kin Hubbard, "is just about as profitable as bein' a good whittler." Wrong. Knowing a lot (no one knows all) about baseball confers not only the profit of an elevating pleasure, but also that of instruction. It teaches a general truth about excellence. . . .

I am a layman who has spent some time trespassing—respectfully—on the turf of specialists, the men and women who write about baseball full time. I am by vocation a commentator on social events, trends and problems. People who do what I do in periodic journalism often seem to be professional scolds. My interest . . . has been to have fun exploring the spirit and practice and ethic of something fun, a sport. But I can not forbear from drawing a lesson.

The national pastime is better than ever in almost every way and is getting even better every year. The same can not be said about the nation. . . .

American Laziness

I believe America's real problem is individual understretch, a tendency of Americans to demand too little of themselves, at their lathes, their desks, their computer terminals. The baseball men I have spent time with . . . demonstrate an admirable seriousness about their capabilities. They also demonstrate the compatibility of seriousness and fun. In fact, what makes baseball especially fun is seeing the way its best players apply their seriousness.

> *A nation's preferred forms of recreation are not of trivial importance.*

A generation ago a wit said that Americans most wanted to read books about animals or the Civil War, so the ideal book would be *I Was Lincoln's Vet*. Nowadays it sometimes seems that Americans are most interested in "how-to" books, especially those that teach one how to attain thin thighs quickly or sexual ecstasy slowly. Today the shelves in bookstores groan beneath the weight of books purporting to explain how to attain excellence in business, and especially how to beat the Japanese in commercial competition. I will not belabor the point but I do assert it: If Americans made goods and services the way [Cal] Ripken makes double plays, [Tony] Gwynn makes hits, [Orel] Hershiser makes pitches and [Tony] La Russa makes decisions, you would hear no more about the nation's trajectory having passed its apogee.[1]

Enjoying the Game Intelligently

America, the first modern nation, has led the world in what historian Daniel Boorstin calls "mass producing the moment." We do this with photographs, movies, tapes, records, compact disks and copying machines. Modern manufacturing is the mass production of identical products. In merchandising, the development of franchising (McDonald's, Holiday Inns) has made it possible to go from coast to coast having identical experiences eating and sleeping. You can go all the way on the interstate highway system and never really see the particularities of a town. A sport like baseball, although a small universe of rule-regulated behavior, is actually a refreshing realm of diversity. The games are like snowflakes. They are perishable and no one is exactly like any other. But to see the diversities of snowflakes you must look closely and carefully. Baseball, more than any other sport, is enjoyed by the knowledgeable. The pleasures it gives to fans are proportional to the fans' sense of history. Its beauties are visible to the trained eye, which is the result of a long apprenticeship in appreciation. The more such apprenticeships we have, the more we will be able to drive away one of the retrograde features of today's baseball experience, the multiplication of irrelevant sights and sounds in ballparks.

When Roger Angell of *The New Yorker* first decorously expressed his disapproval of Houston's Astrodome, he said that the most common complaint about the place is valid but incidental. The most common complaint is that going to a game there amounts to exchanging your living room for a larger one. But what matters most, Angell said, is the violence done by the entire ambiance of the Astrodome. It is violence

---

1. Ripken, Gwynn and Hershiser are retired. La Russa was the manager for the St. Louis Cardinals team that won the National League pennant in 2004.

done to "the quality of baseball time." A person absorbed in a baseball game should be "in a green place of removal" where tension is intensified slowly, pitch by pitch. The contest has its own continuum and that continuum is degraded by attempts to "use up" time with planned distractions such as entertaining scoreboards, dancing ball girls, costumed mascots and the like. The attempt to attract fans by planned distractions is worse than gilding the lily. It attacks the lily by disregarding its virtue. Baseball's foremost virtue as a spectator sport is that, as Angell says, it "is perhaps the most perfectly visible sport ever devised." That is why it is the sport that most rewards the fan's attention to details and nuances. Nuances should matter to the observer because they matter so much to the participants—managers and players—who determine who wins.

> **❝** *Baseball is a game where you have to do more than one thing very well, but one thing at a time.* **❞**

Bart Giamatti, speaking with Roger Angell, deplored "the NFL-ization of baseball." He meant the infestation of ballparks by clownish mascots (the bastard children of the San Diego Chicken) and the pollution of the parks' atmospheres by "dot races," rock music trivia quizzes and other distractions. Some franchises, said Giamatti, "are like theatrical companies who only want to do Shakespeare in motorcycle boots and leather jackets. They've given up on the beautiful language." The language should suffice. Perhaps NFL-ization is a concession to the "television babies," those Americans under 40 who find rock videos pleasurable and even, in some sense, intelligible. Baseball is a sport for the literate, and not merely in the sense that it involves, for the aficionado, a lot of reading and has frequently been the subject of literature. It is also a mode of expression more suited to a literary than a pictorial culture. A baseball game is an orderly experience—perhaps too orderly for the episodic mentalities of television babies. A baseball game is, like a sentence, a linear sequence; like a paragraph, it proceeds sequentially. But to enjoy it you have to be able to read it. Baseball requires baseball literacy.

It's the Little Things

"This ain't a football game," said Orioles manager Earl Weaver. "We do this every day." That is why baseball is a game you can not play with your teeth clenched. But neither can you play it with your mind idling in neutral. Baseball is a game where you have to do more than one thing very well, but one thing at a time. The best baseball people are (although you do not hear this description bandied about in dugouts) Cartesians. That is, they apply [French philosopher René] Descartes's methods to their craft, breaking it down into bite-size components, mastering them and then building the craft up, bit by bit. Descartes, whose vocation was to think about thinking, said (I am paraphrasing somewhat): The problem is that we make mistakes. The solution is to strip our thought processes down to basics and begin with a rock-solid foundation, some certainty from which we can reason carefully to other certainties. His bedrock certainty was *Cogito ergo sum*—"I think, therefore I am." His theory was that by assembling small certainties, one could build an unassailable edifice of truths. As any infielder could have told Descartes, errors will happen, no matter how careful you are. But Descartes's method is not a bad model of how best to get on with things in life: Master enough little problems and you will have few big problems.

Dizzy Dean once said after a 1-0 game, "The game was closer than the score indicated." In a sense it may well have been. Games are often decided by marginal moves and episodes less stark and noticeable than a run. They are won, and championship seasons are achieved, by the attention to small matters, and the law of cumulation. In the 1952 musical *Pajama Game* there is a song about a wage increase:

> Seven and a half cents doesn't mean a hell of a lot,
> Seven and a half cents doesn't mean a thing,
> But give it to me every hour, forty hours every week,
> And that's enough for me to be living like a king,
> I figured it out.

Ray Kroc, the founder of McDonald's, figured it out. Sell enough 15-cent hamburgers (which is what they cost in the 1950s) and you are a billionaire. Do enough 15-cent things right in baseball—"It breaks down to its smallest parts," Rick Dempsey said—and you may win. Let those parts slide and try to rely on $100 achievements—spectacular events—and you will lose. The best players pay the most attention to baseball's parts. Frank Crosetti, a Yankee coach, saw every game DiMaggio played and never saw him thrown out going from first to third. When DiMaggio was asked why he placed such a high value on excellence he said, "There is always some kid who may be seeing me for the first or last time. I owe him my best."

DiMaggio's dignity was bound up with his brand of excellence. "People said, 'You're so relaxed on the ball field.' I'd say, 'But I knew what I was doing.'" There is also dignity in honest mediocrity, even in the unforgiving meritocracy of professional sports. And there is our obligation for special discipline on the part of the especially gifted. . . .

Work Ethic

Past performance gives rise to averages, on which managers calculate probabilities about performances to come. The more you study, the less surprised you are. But no matter how hard you study, you are still surprised agreeably often. And the surprises that come to the studious are especially delicious. One reason for surprises is that no one puts batteries in the players: They are not robots. They are people whose personalities and characters vary under pressure, including the most important pressure, that which they put on themselves. [Psychologist] William James knew what baseball people know: "There is very little difference between one man and another; but what little there is is very important." All players who make it to the major leagues are superior athletes. The different degrees of superiority in terms of natural physical skills are less marked and less important than another difference. It is the difference in the intensity of the application to the craftsmanship of baseball. Some people work harder than others, a lot harder.

> *Some people work harder than others, a lot harder.*

Standing in the manager's office in Baltimore's Memorial Stadium late on a Sunday afternoon in the middle of June, 1989, and in the dishevelment of a man eager to get out of uniform and out of town, Tony La Russa, manager of the Oakland

Athletics, was being asked why the Orioles, recently such lowly wretches, were playing so well. They had just beaten the Athletics three times in three days. What was the secret? Was it pitching? Defense? Neither, said La Russa, his natural curtness now compounded with impatience at journalistic obtuseness. The secret, he said, clipping every word like a fuse, is no secret. It is at the core of all baseball success. It is intensity: "They are playing hard."

> **" Those who pay the price of excellence in any demanding discipline are heroes. "**

Intensity in athletics has many manifestations. As a youngster, Pete Maravich dribbled a basketball wherever he walked, and sometimes while sitting. At movies he selected aisle seats so he could bounce the ball during the show. The young Ted Williams walked around San Diego squeezing a rubber ball to develop his forearms. After the Yankees lost the 1960 World Series on Bill Mazeroski's ninth-inning home run over the left-field wall in Forbes Field, Mickey Mantle wept during the entire flight back to New York. It sometimes seems odd, or even perverse, that intensity—the engagement of the passions—should matter in professional athletics. To some people this seems inexplicable now that players are pulling down such princely sums. Tommy Lasorda, [former] manager of the Los Angeles Dodgers, is known as a good baseball mind and an extraordinary motivator. He is often asked if it is really necessary to motivate someone making a million dollars. Damn right, says Lasorda. To most people, the word "motivate," when used in an athletic context, means to inflame players the way Knute Rockne is said to have aroused his teams at Notre Dame. Lasorda is quite capable of that. He can be an exquisitely profane Pericles (if that is not too oxymoronic). But that is not the heart of the matter. In a baseball context, to motivate is to maintain the cool concentration and discipline necessary for maximum performance during six months of competition in a game especially unforgiving of minor mistakes.

It is the everydayness of baseball that demands of the player a peculiar equilibrium, a balance of relaxation and concentration. One afternoon, during Andre Dawson's 1987 MVP season, he was in right field in Wrigley Field and the Cubs were clobbering the Astros, 11-1. In the top of the sixth inning Dawson ran down a foul fly, banging into the brick wall that is right next to the foul line. In the seventh inning he charged and made a sliding catch on a low line drive that otherwise would have been an unimportant single. When asked after the game why he would risk injuries in those situations when the outcome of the game was not in doubt, Dawson replied laconically, "Because the ball was in play." Dawson probably found the question unintelligible. The words and syntax were clear enough but the questioner obviously was oblivious to the mental (and moral) world of a competitor like Dawson. . . . Baseball heroism is not a matter of flashes of brilliance; rather, it is the quality of (in [writer] John Updike's words) "the players who always *care*," about themselves and their craft. . . .

Hero Appreciation vs. Hero Worship

We live in a relentlessly antiheroic age. Perhaps in a democratic culture there always is a leveling impulse, a desire to cut down those who rise. Today, however, there also seems to be a small minded, mean-spirited resentment of those who rise, a reluctance to give credit where it is due, a flinching from unstinting admiration, a desire to disbelieve in the rewarded virtue of the few. We have a swamp of journalism suited to such an age, a journalism infused with a corrosive, leveling spirit.

Yet it has been said that no man is a hero to his valet, not because no man is a hero but because all valets are valets. It requires a certain largeness of spirit to give generous appreciation to large achievements. A society with a crabbed spirit and a cynical urge to discount and devalue will find that one day, when it needs to draw upon the reservoirs of excellence, the reservoirs have run dry. A society in which the capacity for warm appreciation of excellence atrophies will find that its capacity for excellence diminishes. Happiness, too, diminishes as the appreciation of excellence diminishes. That is no small loss, least of all to a nation in which the pursuit of happiness was endorsed in the founding moment.

America has been called the only nation founded on a good idea. That idea has been given many and elaborate explanations, but the most concise and familiar formulation is the pursuit of happiness. For a fortunate few people, happiness is the pursuit of excellence in a vocation. The vocation can be a profession or a craft, elite or common, poetry or carpentry. What matters most is an idea of excellence against which to measure achievement. The men whose careers are considered here exemplify the pursuit of happiness through excellence in a vocation. Fortunate people have a talent for happiness. Possession of any talent can help a person toward happiness. As Aristotle said, happiness is not a condition that is produced or stands on its own; rather, it is a frame of mind that accompanies an activity. But another frame of mind comes first. It is a steely determination to do well.

When Ted Williams, the last .400 hitter, arrived in Boston for his first season he said, with the openness of a Westerner and the innocence of a 20-year-old, "All I want out of life is that when I walk down the street folks will say, 'There goes the greatest hitter who ever lived.'" Today, if you see Williams walking down the street and you say, "There goes the greatest hitter who ever lived," you may get an argument but you will not get derision. He won 6 batting titles and lost another by one hit. (In 1949 George Kell batted .3429, Williams .3427.) He batted .406 in 1941 and .388 in 1957, when his 38-year-old legs surely cost him at least the 3 hits that would have given him his second .400 season.[2]

The hard blue glow from people like Williams lights the path of progress in any field. I said at the outset that this was to be an antiromantic look at baseball. I meant that baseball is work. Baseball is hard and demands much drudgery. But it is neither romantic nor sentimental to say that those who pay the price of excellence in any demanding discipline are heroes. Cool realism recognizes that they are necessary. As a character says in Bernard Malamud's baseball novel *The Natural*, when we are without heroes we "don't know how far we can go."

2. Ted Williams died in 2002.

6

Black Athletes Are Unfairly Expected to Behave Like White Role Models

Todd Boyd

Todd Boyd is the author of several books, including Am I Black Enough for You? Popular Culture from the 'Hood and Beyond. *He has appeared on many television shows as a popular media commentator. Boyd is also a professor of critical studies at the USC School of Cinema-Television.*

Many young African American players in the NBA are held to a double standard: They are expected to behave, not complain about their pay, and just be grateful that they have the chance to play, while white players, coaches, and owners are not held to these same standards. Asking black players to behave as traditional role models is really just a way of telling them to know their place. However, black players in the NBA today, unlike previous generations of African American athletes, know that they are the reason people are paying to come watch games and believe they should be allowed to have a say in how the NBA does things.

Like the league itself, the NBA draft over the last few years has tended to foreshadow things to come. With [Chinese player] Yao Ming headlining the class of 2002, the global implications for the game and the attendant issues of cultural identity are front and center. The 2001 draft offered another example of the way the game is changing and how this change reflects larger concerns. The Washington Wizards used their first pick in the 2001 draft to select Kwame Brown, a high school player out of Atlanta. Brown was followed by Tyson Chandler, a high school star straight outta Compton, California. With the fourth pick the Chicago Bulls selected another high school star, Eddie Curry. This meant that three of the first four picks in the 2001 draft were high school players. The trend of drafting young players has gotten to be so popular now that LeBron James, the latest addition to the young, Black, rich and famous, was already being predicted to be the first pick in the 2003 draft when he was still a junior in high school.[1]

Though many high schoolers have excelled in the league, none of them had ever been the very first pick in the draft until Brown was picked in 2001. Kwame Brown and the subsequent selection of the other high school players was the culmination of a trend that had been on the upswing for quite some time. . . .

Backlash

Now that this trend is in place, there suddenly seems to be a backlash against the young players who immediately command large sums of money the minute they get drafted. There have been racially loaded questions asked about the appropriateness of making millionaires out of people who are barely voting age. David Stern, the league's commissioner, has even suggested that the players union institute a minimum age limit that would restrict players under age twenty from competing. This position is supported by many in the media and in society at large. There has always been consternation about the amount of money that Black athletes make, and this has increased. It is now camouflaged as an age issue. Oftentimes those cries about players being too young are really coded discussions about them being too Black.

Interestingly, no one has lodged similar complaints about sports like tennis or gymnastics, where participants often start competing nationally and internationally at an even earlier age than they do in basketball. Tennis, for example, tends to be

---

1. James was taken as the first pick by the Cleveland Cavaliers and went on to win the NBA's "Rookie of the Year" award.

more White and middle- to upper-middle-class in its orientation, the amazing Venus and Serena Williams notwithstanding. There is no threat to the status quo if a young middle-class White girl like Jennifer Capriati or upper-middle-class figure like Lindsay Davenport starts to make millions on the tennis court. Young middle-class or upper-middle-class White girls with no college education have for years been dominant and financially successful on the tennis court. Yet there is a sense that it is wrong or poses some threat when a young Black man from the 'hood attempts to do the same on the basketball court.

> *There have been racially loaded questions asked about the appropriateness of making millionaires out of people who are barely voting age.*

The possibility of an age limit in the NBA speaks to this directly. If enacted, it would represent an overt attempt to forestall the money-making capabilities of young Black men. Though the WTA [Women's Tennis Association], which governs woman's pro tennis, has now instituted the so-called "Capriati rule," the age limit is still set at only fifteen, much younger than the age limit of twenty that the NBA is suggesting. This argument about an age limit, in the NBA is often shrouded in discussions of "what's best for the kids" or "what's best for the game." This effort to deny economic opportunity is a direct challenge to financial aspirations of potential NBA stars and an overt attempt to prohibit young Black men from becoming rich and famous.

Locked Out

During the 1998 off-season, the NBA and the players union engaged in a very public battle over a new collective bargaining agreement that would govern player contracts and league finances. Consensus would suggest that the NBA won that battle decisively. More important, the league was able to cast the players association as the bad guy in the negotiations by making it appear as though the players were "on strike" as opposed to being "locked out" by the owners, which was the case. By locking out the players, the NBA had in effect forced a work stoppage that resulted in a long portion of the season being canceled until the two sides reached an agreement. The players association, in a largely futile attempt to counter perceptions, took out ads in many major publications declaring that they had been locked out as opposed to being on strike.

> *Oftentimes those cries about players being too young are really coded discussions about them being too Black.*

There is a big difference between the two positions. To be locked out means that the league does not allow the players to make a living while they are negotiating. To be on strike means that the players themselves decide to stop work. Amid the antiunion atmosphere that has flourished in this country since Ronald Reagan fired all those striking air traffic controllers back in the '80s, this sentiment, coupled with the resentment many feel toward wealthy Black athletes anyway, was quite a lethal combination. The players association emerged from the episode looking greedy and concerned only with advancing their own selfish interests.

The public meanwhile was ready to accept the worst possible interpretation of the players' behavior. Many feel that the players make too much money anyway. So it was common during this time to hear people say that they did not care much about a group of millionaires who wanted more money than most working people would ever make in their lives. This appeal to class bias worked and helped paint the union membership, the overwhelming majority of whom were Black, as avaricious and mercenary.

The Real Moneymakers

On the other hand, people never seem to complain about how much money NBA owners make. No one seems concerned that NBA commissioner David Stern makes a multimillion-dollar salary himself, for that matter. The public certainly does not begrudge or resent the owners' right to make money or the commissioner's right to be compensated at such a high salary for carrying out the owners' bidding.

Billionaire owners like Paul Allen, the cofounder of Microsoft, who also owns the Portland Trail Blazers, or Howard Schultz, who owns Starbucks and the Seattle SuperSonics, are never told that they already have too much money, so their NBA earnings should and will be capped. This would be inconceivable, as these individuals are allowed to make as much money as they possibly can and indeed, are celebrated, respected, and admired for doing it. . . .

In order for these owners to pay such large sums to the players, however, they must make even larger sums. This seems not to be a problem. The owners are entitled to make as much as they want without fear of reprisal. The players, by contrast, who "own" their ability and who draw the fans to the arenas and television screens, are thought to be taking money that they do not deserve, almost as though they are stealing it. Racial stereotypes are abundant in these perceptions: it is acceptable for a White billionaire to make money off of Black athletic labor, but it is not acceptable for a Black athlete to profit from his own talents and labors.

> *People never seem to complain about how much money NBA owners make.*

The owners can charge exorbitant ticket prices because of the talent the players bring to bear. Global corporations and wealthy individuals spend large sums to buy courtside tickets to watch basketball, again, because of the players. No fan has ever gone to a basketball game to *see* someone "coach," nor have they gone to a game to *see* someone "own." People attend basketball games and watch on television to see players do what they do best, play the game. Yet when these players attempt to discuss the circumstances around their working conditions, they are treated as greedy villains trying to destroy the American way of life and sporting tradition when indeed, they are simply behaving like capitalists of the highest order.

It is almost as though because they make so much money they should not even be allowed to complain about labor issues, even though these issues persist, even though they are important considerations. The underlying assumption here, when considering the racial implications, is that these Black players should be grateful for the mere opportunity to earn the money in the first place. The imposition of this notion, which stipulates that one "needs to be grateful," is where America's true colors, no pun intended, are quite visible.

The Hip Hop Influence

As the players in question get to be younger and younger, it is certain that the influence of hip hop will continue to reign supreme. Hip hop at this point is more than just the music that the players listen to on their ubiquitous headphones, in the same way that basketball is more than just another game. Hip hop is a way of life that best defines the worldview from which these contemporary players emerge.

Hip hop has always been about having an upward trajectory. An abiding sense of social mobility abounds. Basketball has become the way that many who are talented enough and fortunate enough get to experience that mobility. This is their opportunity to showcase their skills and become rich in the process. What angers and alarms so many is the fact that a lot of these players have no interest whatsoever in imitating the ways of mainstream White society. This is evident in the style choices favored by so many contemporary players. Cornrows have replaced the bald head. Long baggy shorts are de rigueur. Tattoos are the order of the day.

> *Unlike others, Black men are not allowed to exhibit anything remotely approximating passion.*

The exception to this is a player like Tim Duncan, he of West Indian descent. West Indians have often been considered as better able to assimilate into mainstream America than their African American counterparts; think Sidney Poitier and Colin Powell, for example. Duncan then seems to be a throwback, a player from a previous time whose fundamental style of play and extremely unassuming disposition make him stand out among a league of players deeply ensconced in the hip hop milieu. No matter how much attention is lavished on Duncan by approving league and media starmakers, he is the exception, not the rule. Hip hop–minded players dominate the game and the conversations around it.

Though Duncan may be a throwback, it is a player like Rasheed Wallace who to me epitomizes the idea of retro. Wallace alternates between cornrows and a nappy old-school 'fro, also in the signature shoe of the hip hop generation, the now vintage Nike Air Force One. Wallace has also been a source of controversy throughout his tenure in the league. He was one of the first players that the league fined for wearing his shorts too long, for instance.

Obviously the length of someone's shorts has nothing to do with how he plays basketball. A player wearing long shorts does not in any way gain a competitive advantage over a player in shorter pants. As the length of all basketball shorts has gotten longer over time, the extremely long shorts are about style, and especially hip hop style. This is where the problem comes in. The NBA wants to control the players' image and suppress expression of this hip hop style on the court. The result is the enforcement of nonsensical rules about ultimately insignificant issues like the length of shorts.

> **Allen Iverson did not grow up in the same world that Joe Louis did, and he has not had the same experiences either.**

John Stockton, the older White superstar of the Utah Jazz, continues to wear his shorts at the same length they were worn back in the old days. His especially "short shorts" are worn to make a statement that he is not like the younger Black players in the league. Stockton's shorts are like basketball's version of the Confederate flag; an attempt to hold on to an antiquated and outdated sense of the NBA in spite of the obvious changes that abound. [Stockton retired after the 2003 season.]

Many of the younger Black players in the league, like Rasheed Wallace, wear their shorts long to make an equally provocative statement: "This is our league, and we will do things in accordance with our culture." Early in the 2001–2002 season, several Black players, including Kobe Bryant and Shaquille O'Neal, were fined and told to make the length of their shorts conform to league standards.

Hip hop–minded players like Rasheed Wallace are constantly being criticized for other things as well. The media has tended to focus on Wallace's excessive number of technical fouls, of which admittedly there are many. Wallace's emotion on the court is a demonstration of his desire to play the game at a high level. No one knows what to do with a Black man who exhibits emotion though. Unlike others, Black men are not allowed to exhibit anything remotely approximating passion. It is too often misperceived as a violent threat. In this regard they seem to be caught in a frustrating catch-22. If someone is angry, they are too emotional. And if they are laid back, they are not angry enough.

Double Standards

This double standard was most clearly at work when Rasheed Wallace was called for a technical foul in a playoff game against the Lakers back in 2000. Wallace was charged with a technical for an "intimidating stare" pointed in the direction of referee Ron Garretson. Though Wallace's reputation of being given to outbursts preceded him, this call was ridiculous. The call was the equivalent of accusing Wallace of "reckless eyeballing," a Jim Crow charge often leveled against Black men when it was perceived that they had been looking at a White woman or looking in a way thought disrespectful to a White person.

Though players like Wallace have come to represent the majority of players in the league, they are often still being discussed and manipulated by people of another generation and from another disposition altogether. Gone are the days when Jackie Robinson broke the color line in baseball and Black athletes were simply content to be included. Things have now changed quite drastically. One cannot honestly discuss sports in American society without including the contributions of Black people as a primary part of that conversation. After several generations of prominent Black athletes, their significance in sports is very much like their significance in the music industry: unquestionable. These are two areas of the culture where Black people have not only excelled, but where they are the standard by which all others are measured.

This being the case, contemporary Black athletes feel no need to simply be content because they are being included. Unfortunately, their inclusion on the athletic side of things often mirrors a relative exclusion in other realms of the sporting world. Many members of the mainstream media are White and of a different generation. They often want to impose the dictates of the past on the Black athletes of the present. They tend to have the same expectations of an Allen Iverson as they did of a Joe Louis. Allen Iverson did not grow up in the same world that Joe Louis did, and he has not had the same experiences either. So why should he be expected to think and act in the same way? Contemporary Black basketball players have a great deal of money at their disposal along with a great deal of visibility and power. Yet the people who tend to control the aspects of the game off the court—the media, the league—reflect these old ideas and expectations.

Young, Black, Rich and Famous

I have often found that the incongruity of these circumstances is best reflected in the term "role model." To me, this is a modern-day version of saying that someone is a "credit to their race," as they said about Joe Louis and others in the past. Role model is another way of saying to the young, Black, rich and famous, "Stay in your place, speak when spoken to, and do as you are told . . . be thankful for what you've got." In response, the young, Black, rich and famous raise an extended middle finger. This seems to have resulted in an impasse. The proverbial unstoppable force meets the immovable object.

What emboldens the young, Black, rich and famous is that they know they are the reason people are paying attention in the first place. They are the reason for being. This reflects a shift in power relations. This is not to say that Black basketball players run things, but they do have a say-so. They are the attraction and they are the straws that stir the drink. Like stars in Hollywood who draw people to their movies, these basketball players command the box office. When the media, the establishment, and those fans with their heads in the sand wake up, they will realize all of this too. You cannot force a Black square peg into a round White hole. You cannot draw White blood from a Black turnip. You can however turn the game of basketball into a global entertainment commodity, with Black players at the center of a new definition of what now constitutes America.

7

Football Players Are Poor Role Models Because So Many Commit Crimes

Jeff Benedict and Don Yaeger

Jeff Benedict is an investigative reporter and the author of several books, including Public Heroes, Private Felons: Athletes and Crimes Against Women. *He is the former director of research at the Center for the Study of Sport in Society at Northeastern University. Don Yaeger is an editor and writer for* Sports Illustrated *and is the author of several books, including* Under the Tarnished Dome.

A 1998 survey of the National Football League (NFL) showed that at least 21 percent of players in the league had been charged with a serious crime, yet none of these players had been disciplined or suspended by the NFL. The NFL argues that there is no evidence that its players are any more likely to commit crimes than their non-NFL "peers," but this misses the point. Professional athletes receive great financial rewards and are looked up to as role models. They should therefore be held to a higher standard.

It's no secret that NFL teams draft players who have had run-ins with the law, even players who have served time. (As long as they are "players," of course.) And why not, the logic goes. These guys are not being drafted into the Boy Scouts of Amer-

Jeff Benedict and Don Yaeger, *Pros and Cons: The Criminals Who Play in the NFL.* New York: Warner Books, Inc., 1998. Copyright © 1998 by Jeff Benedict and Don Yaeger. All rights reserved. Reproduced by permission of the publisher.

ica. This is pro football. Besides, if you listen to coaches and NFL team spokespersons, these past "indiscretions of youth" are not serious crimes. Consider Dick Vermeil's comments after drafting Ryan Tucker. "First off," Vermeil explained to the press, "character guys get in fights from time to time, especially when they didn't start it. I like the guys that don't start it but finish it. I like those kind of guys. This is a physical contact game. . . . But we've got a ton of guys in the National Football League that have some true character problems. I don't believe this guy does." Of course not. What coach wouldn't try to minimize the negative public exposure that his team may face when drafting a violent criminal?

Another popular excuse used by team and league officials to justify the drafting of criminally convicted players goes something like this: as long as these players have served their jail time, it would be unfair to deny them an opportunity to earn a living and become productive members of society. After all, what adult wants to be judged on the basis of the follies of adolescence?

Sounds fair enough. But with mottos like "Just Win Baby," how far will NFL teams go to rationalize giving players with checkered pasts a new lease on life? Will they forgive a habitual criminal offender if he can run a 4.3 forty? Or draft a violent felon because he can bench-press over 500 pounds? How about a drug dealer? A convicted sex offender? A member of a violent street gang? An accused killer?

The evidence suggests the answer is yes to all of the above.

In researching this book, the authors identified 509 players [in 1998] whose criminal records could be checked in two states or more. Of these 509 players, an amazing 109 had been formally charged with a serious crime.

Not Taking a Stand

With NFL Commissioner Paul Tagliabue's recent strong public stance against players' off-field deviance, one might wonder how many of the players in the authors' survey[1] were kicked out of the league.

Answer: zero.

The closest Tagliabue has come to taking a stand against a criminal player was in 1990. Four years earlier, backup offen-

---

1. The authors checked a sample of roughly one-third of the players on NFL rosters for the 1996 and 1997 seasons and carried out criminal records checks on them.

sive lineman Kevin Allen was cut from the Philadelphia Eagles due to poor performance. Days later, he raped a woman and was arrested. After serving thirty-three months in jail following his conviction, he petitioned the league for the opportunity to play again. Tagliabue denied the petition, saying, "The public perception of [Allen's] being released from prison and then being allowed to return to football is very negative, and there's validity in the perception. There is a negative public reaction to NFL players who engage in criminal conduct and then are allowed to re-enter the league."

> *What coach wouldn't try to minimize the negative public exposure that his team may face when drafting a violent criminal?*

The commissioner's stand against a journeyman lineman rings hollow considering the number of other players *in the league today* who have served time in jail or prison for serious crimes. And his statement in the Allen case flies in the face of the league's more commonly stated approach toward criminal conduct. "We're not the criminal justice system," NFL spokesperson Greg Aiello told the *Washington Post* in 1994. "We can't cure every ill in society. You know, we're putting on football games. And unless it impacts on the business, we have to be very careful [from a legal standpoint] about disciplinary action we take. A player has rights too."

Unless, of course, he gambles. This misdemeanor offense will get a player banned right quick, and there will be little clamoring from the NFL about due process. Why? Because gambling, like steroids, gives the image of an artificial on-field product, which has a direct correlation to, as Aiello said, the "business" of the NFL. Violent crime, on the other hand, apparently does not.

Multiple Arrests

Together, the 109 players who showed up in the authors' survey with a criminal history had been arrested a combined 264 times. That's an average of 2.42 arrests per player.

Keep in mind that the 264 arrests involve only the most serious offenses. Although the authors discovered a substantial number of players who had been charged with minor misdemeanors (credit card theft, shoplifting, urinating in public, disturbing the peace, etc.) and traffic offenses (speeding and driving with a suspended license), none of these offenses are included in the authors' statistics. The intent was to deal strictly with the more serious criminals in the NFL and the very serious crimes they commit.

A breakdown of the 264 arrests shows:

2 for homicide

7 for rape

4 for kidnapping

45 for domestic violence

42 for aggravated assault/assault and battery (nondomestic violence cases)

25 for other crimes against persons, including robbery and armed robbery

15 for drug crimes, including intent to distribute cocaine, possession of cocaine, and possession of marijuana

32 for crimes against property, including fraud, larceny, burglary, theft, and property destruction

35 for driving under the influence of alcohol or drugs

17 for resisting arrest

40 for other public safety crimes, including illegal use or possession of a weapon and trespassing. (Note: Trespassing was included only when connected to a domestic violence complaint or an incident involving multiple defendants where someone was charged with a more serious offense.)

As astonishing as these numbers are, it may well be only the tip of the iceberg, albeit an iceberg of *Titanic* proportions. Challenges posed by restrictive public access laws, a near-complete block-out of juvenile criminal records, and the transient nature of NFL players made it impossible to have a complete accounting of all NFL players' criminal histories.

For example, Oakland Raiders running back Derrick Fenner, who *is* among the 509 players whose history was checked by the authors, was charged with murder in 1987 in Washington, D.C. (He was ultimately exonerated.) This arrest does not show up in the authors' statistics because the District of Columbia is not among the jurisdictions that provided criminal history records to the authors.

In all, the authors discovered over fifty additional players whose criminal histories *as adults* included serious crimes. But these players were *not* included in the authors' statistics because their crimes were discovered by methods that failed to meet the strict standard set for inclusion in the database. . . . (In other words, records checks were done in only one state or in a state where the players resided for less than five years.)

Put simply, the number of crimes (264) and criminals (109) recorded here are conservative.

Athletes vs. Plumbers

"Have you done a study asking how many serious crimes are committed by a group of 1,700 lawyers or 1,700 plumbers?" asked Aiello, when contacted by the authors for this book. "How are you supposed to know if this [21 percent of the players formally charged with serious crimes] is unusual?"

Yes, all this data begs the question: Are professional athletes in general or NFL players in particular more prone to criminal behavior than the general population? The answer depends on who you compare them to. If you compare them to their ethnic, demographic, and economic "peers"—adult males under thirty-two who have completed college and earn at least six-figure salaries (of the 509 players in the survey, all earn over $150,000 per year—the minimum salary in the NFL—and most earn considerably more, and virtually all attended four years of college)—NFL players would clearly be overrepresented. Typically, college-educated, high-income earners do not commit violent crime.

> *Will they forgive a habitual criminal offender if he can run a 4.3 forty?*

However, it is somewhat misleading to compare professional football players to others who complete college and earn salaries comparable to those of NFL players. Why? First, unlike NFL players individuals earnings six- and seven-figure salaries are generally not employed to engage in violence for a living. Second, very few people who obtain college degrees and earn NFL-like salaries come from backgrounds similar to those of many NFL players. For starters, 78 percent of the 509 players in the authors' survey are black. (This figure is consistent with the overall percentage of blacks in the NFL, which was 67 percent during the 1996–97 season.) The research revealed that a fair number of these players come from disadvantaged backgrounds.

Disadvantaged?

Yet, some point out that it is inappropriate to compare NFL players to men from disadvantaged backgrounds. Most people who grow up in "disadvantaged" circumstances are not given the opportunity to receive a free college education, earn millions of dollars, and become celebrated citizens. Given that NFL players have extraordinary earning opportunities, conventional wisdom suggests they would be less inclined to turn to crime in college for fear of risking all those potential millions as pros. Further, logic dictates that once they enter the NFL, pros would be even less likely to commit crimes because they have so much at stake were they to be convicted.

Neither of these theories were supported by the authors' findings. Of the 109 players who had been charged with a serious crime, thirty-two were arrested *before* entering the NFL, sixty-one were arrested *after* entering the NFL, and sixteen had been arrested both *before and after* joining the NFL.

> *Individuals earning six- and seven-figure salaries are generally not employed to engage in violence for a living.*

The reason, it seems, for this break from conventional wisdom is simple. Virtually every other profession that pays employees NFL-like salaries would hardly recruit criminals. Even fewer would retain workers who commit serious crimes after being hired. And those who earn six- and seven-figure salaries are, at least in part, discouraged from participating in serious crime by the knowledge that to act in that manner would jeopardize the wealth and freedom they enjoy.

But nothing in the data suggests that criminal activity puts an NFL player's career in jeopardy. Why worry about breaking the law if there is no real risk of losing your millions? The old saying "Crime doesn't pay" reads a little differently for NFL players. "If you can *play*, you don't have to pay."

Expectations for Role Models

The NFL may continue to argue that there is no scientific study proving that its players are disproportionately involved in crime. This posture, however, is slouching under the weight of recurring arrests of players. And this fact remains: at least 21 percent of the men from the most visible class of role models in America have been charged with a serious crime—an average of nearly two and half times per arrested player. To ask for statistical proof that they are worse than the other criminals in society as a prerequisite for doing something about it is to ask the wrong question.

"That should not be the context or basis by which you make your policy," explained former U.S. Education Secretary and Drug Czar William Bennett in an interview. . . . "You make your policy based on the laws of the land, on the expectation you have for your athletes, on the recognition that they are role models for young people—whether we like it or not. It's natural for boys, in particular, to look up to these big, fast, strong men. They have a larger place in a child's imagination and aspirations than the posse of heroes from other categories. They dominate the stage. They are who kids are looking at most. So what they do is critical. They have the possibility for encouraging or discouraging responsible behavior.

"As a result, the expectation of standards ought to be higher for professional athletes," Bennett continued, "because of the public nature of their profession—the high salaries, public exposure, and adulation. With all the benefits comes responsibility. The fact that some of these criminals are getting a waiver because they are athletes not only corrupts sports, it corrupts the legal system. So, ask the right questions and look in the right places."

Besides, focusing on whether athletes are any worse than other criminals really misses the more noteworthy point—that professional football players are rarely held accountable for their crimes or stigmatized for their actions due to their athleticism. Simply put, the NFL's criminal players are treated differently than virtually every other criminal who commits similar crimes.

8

Female Athletes Encourage Girls and Women to Develop Confidence

Marian Betancourt

Marian Betancourt is the author of more than a dozen books, including What to Do When Love Turns Violent: A Resource for Women in Abusive Relationships. *She is a member of the Women's Sports Foundation.*

Sports offer adolescent girls the opportunity to gain self-esteem at a time in their lives when they often lose it. Through sports, girls and young women learn that their bodies are not simply a source of beauty for men to admire. Instead of trying to attain the prevailing body type portrayed in the media, they focus on developing strength and pride in their bodies. Studies show that girls and young women who participate in sports are less likely than their nonathletic classmates to engage in dangerous or harmful activities. Female athletes learn lessons through sports that help them throughout their lives. Sportswomen have found many ways to encourage girls to play and enjoy sports.

A s all of us who have been there know, as a teenager, it is horrible to be different in any way, to not fit in. And while boys have always had their "club" of sports in which to belong, until recently girls did not. So all those surging hormones of adolescence, all that power and energy, was squelched or diverted into waiting for him to call, trying not to beat him at bowling or the math exam, and learning how to dress and flirt. This energy burns inward as obsession with the body's appearance (manifested in bulimia and [anorexia]) instead of the body's power, physical strength, and confidence.

During puberty girls get a suddenly diminished body image that leads to low self-esteem no matter how tall or short they are. If self-consciousness isn't about height, it's about weight, or the shape of a nose, or breasts that are too small or too large. Tall women are told (or get the silent message) they won't find a husband, so they slouch and stoop to hide their height. If a girl's breasts develop out of proportion to the rest of her, she covers them with baggy clothing or carries her books crushed to her chest. The old standard that still exists is that girls and women are judged by their looks. We must be perfect and beautiful or we are not women.

> *Once they are on the floor they see themselves as athletes. They're not worried about their hair or their clothes.*

Little boys see their like images on television and in photos in the sports section and know from their parents and friends that they are expected to play sports. They receive balls, gloves, and sports equipment by the age of two. Research shows that boys and girls between the ages of six and nine—and their parents—are equally interested in sports participation. However, as girls reach puberty, they receive subtle and not-so-subtle messages from everyone around them, and by the age of 14, girls drop out of sports at a significantly greater rate than boys.

Father Figures

But fathers can help change this pattern. Having an encouraging dad around during the teen years does a lot to help girls get through these years of doubts about their body image. A study by researchers at Loyola University of Chicago reveals that girls who are encouraged in sports by their dads are less likely to have eating disorders. Joe Kelly founded Dads and Daughters after one of his daughters asked him if he thought she was fat. Kelly's organization is educating fathers about their role in their daughters' self-esteem. Dads and Daughters also pressures the media to remove advertisements that make girls worry about their looks.

> *The beauty of sports is that it increases self-esteem at an age when girls traditionally lose self-esteem.*

Until recently, girls and women simply did not receive the same opportunities as boys to play or the same positive reinforcement about sports participation. And still, go into any toy store and the first question a clerk will ask you is whether you are shopping for a boy or a girl. If you are browsing in the sports department, you are likely to be asked how big "he" is or what sport "he" plays. Toy stores are divided up into pink and blue. Boys' sections carry sporting goods and lots of toy soldiers and toy guns. Girls' aisles show Barbie and tea sets and toy kitchens and cut-out dolls. While Barbie now has costumes to show that she can be a doctor—even a basketball player—these specialty dolls don't sell nearly as well as the stereotypical Barbie in her shorts and tight shirt.

Some toys, of course, have crossed the gender barrier, but these are mostly computer-geared inventions such as Pokémon and Digimon. *Unisex* may be a big word at the Gap or at your hair-cutting salon, but it just isn't so in the toy stores. Only a few sporting goods stores carry the licensed products of the WNBA [Women's National Basketball Association] or the Women's National Soccer Team—or any teams that are less well known. The good news is that teenaged girls—and many boys—now admire [soccer player] Mia Hamm as much as they admire Michael Jordan. In fact, Nintendo produced the first video game about women's sports, a game that features Mia Hamm, action figure.

Mean Boys

Even when boys attend girls' games, they often stoop to criticizing physical attributes in their taunts and slurs. "Look at those boats," or "Are those skis?" about long feet, they yell from the stands. If a girl has broad shoulders, they might yell for her to go on a diet. Short hair, like a buzz cut, will draw catcalls like, "You got a guy on the team there."

Tamika Catchings, University of Tennessee six feet one junior, has a hearing impairment that meant she had to wear large hearing aids until she was in junior high school. Because the kids teased her, she stopped wearing them. At Tennessee games she always had to ask teammates what coach Pat Summitt was shouting. Now, able to use smaller aids, Catchings is more comfortable with the condition. And she can definitely hear Summitt's yells.

"I still watch myself getting anxious about being feminine," said Joy McCarthy, a psychologist who played sports as a child and in college. She recalled getting ready for a game— the stretching and warm-up exercises. "I was always aware of standing and making sure I looked feminine. But those who play basketball today don't worry about it," she said.

> *I lift weights not so I'll look strong to other people, but so I'll be strong.*

Carole Oglesby recalled a day in her teen years when she was all decked out in Bermuda shorts and new socks and feeling really cool. "Some of the guys commented that I had football legs." Such a remark could have devastated many girls. Fortunately, Oglesby had a supportive family, and so she did not give up her interest in sports. However, like all women who grew up in those dark ages, she understands how girls and young women felt when something they were trying to do was mocked. After all, she remembers that remark to this day. Oglesby did not continue to play softball because there were no opportunities to play at her level of skill; therefore, what was available was not much fun. "I still miss it," she said. However, Oglesby coached softball for a few years after college and directed her physical energy into jogging and skiing.

This self-consciousness of how we look is a big women's issue, even for women who are involved in sports. I doubt many men think about "looking masculine" as they play, but as women, we are so used to being objectified that we do it to ourselves, "watching" ourselves to be sure we're making the "right impression." Involvement in sports can change this because a girl is focused on the game rather than her body.

"Once they are on the floor they see themselves as athletes. They're not worried about their hair or their clothes," said Anna Maria Lopez, athletic director of a Catholic girls' high school in Oregon. "There's something about being able to perform in front of other people." Lopez believes this is easier for girls in a single-sex school. "They have a lot more confidence."

Building Confidence

The beauty of sports is that it increases self-esteem at an age when girls traditionally lose self-esteem. Physical competence creates a sense of self-mastery and strength. A girl can make a decision from a position of strength, something boys learn as small children and carry with them throughout their lives. Whether a boy is short or tall, black or white, if he excels in sports, he is accepted by all.

In the past, exercise for adolescent girls was restricted to gym class or jumping up and down as a cheerleader for the boys' teams who were getting a real physical workout. How many girls were turned on by gym class, with its regimen of calisthenics or aerobics, which had no apparent goal or focus? Not to mention those awful gym suits! In the spirit of adolescent rebellion, they looked for any excuse not to participate. Girls grew up to be sedentary women. However, beating the other team or winning a school championship or getting an athletic scholarship to a good college would interest a girl enough to make physical fitness a big part of her life today—and raise her self-esteem.

> *When you grow up proud of your body and feeling physically strong it stays with you for life.*

A member of the Amherst, Massachusetts, girls' high school basketball team that was portrayed so memorably in Madeleine Blais's book *In These Girls, Hope Is a Muscle* perhaps summed up all that it means to be a teenager and an athlete when she said, "Madonna is not my hero. She wanted attention, she wanted money, she wanted glory, she wanted the microphone, and she did it just by taking off her clothes. I treat my body 360 degrees different. I lift weights not so I'll look strong to other people, but so I'll *be* strong. I take care of my body. I make sure I sleep. I sleep a lot more than my friends. I eat well . . . too much sugar, but other than that I'm fine. If I get an injury like a pull, I listen to it. I don't drink; I don't smoke. I ask enough of my body without asking it to deal with random substances. Once she got hold of the microphone, she just took off more clothes. She never did anything except be sexy. I resent the message that if you are sexy, you are powerful. That's what I think Madonna stands for. As an athlete, it kills me."

On the Court, Out of Trouble

"I was too involved with basketball," said Kathleen Connolly about why she rarely dated. When a boy asked her out in the eighth grade she said, "I've got basketball." This was her reason also for never smoking or doing drugs. "I knew it wasn't good."

A survey released in 1998 by the Women's Sports Foundation found that girls who play sports in school have sex later and don't get pregnant in their teen years as often as girls who are not involved in sports.

According to the President's Council on Physical Fitness and Sports in 1997, female high school athletes tend to get better grades than the girls who are not involved in sports. They are also less likely to drop out of school than girls who are not athletic. They are more likely to go to college and will develop fewer chronic health problems such as heart disease or high cholesterol. The report also indicated that girls who participate in sports are more mentally fit and develop social skills more easily than less-active girls.

"Softball was the first life skill where I learned what it meant to be good at something," said sports psychologist Carole Oglesby, who played softball as a teenager in California.

Lessons for Life

When you grow up proud of your body and feeling physically strong it stays with you for life. Kim Many, a 28-year-old corporate attorney in New York who plays recreational basketball with the New York Urban Professionals Athletic League, said, "I have always played team sports, and I think that it helped to define who I am. I did not have to rely on other things such as how much attention I received from boys or peers in high school because I was always in the [news]paper for my athletic prowess. Without team sports, I would not be the same confident individual that I am today. Excelling in athletics gives me confidence in other areas in my life."

> **" The better I do in athletics, the better I feel about myself. "**

Elizabeth McCarthy, 32, who plays in the same basketball league, said, "When I began playing on my high school team, there was a radical transformation. I didn't feel like an outsider anymore, which I did prior to that. It gave me an identity with a group of fun people and kept me from only being a shy, smart girl. It was also a place where it was not only OK to be tall, it was great, so I think it made me much more comfortable with myself physically."

"The better I do in athletics, the better I feel about myself," said Indiana University volleyball player Laura Mettes, 21. "I definitely have more self-confidence. Being an athlete at a major Division I university defines who you are. People that I don't even know will come up and say 'nice game' or 'I saw you on TV.' At first it was weird, but you get used to it.". . .

Role Models of Transformation

Boys grow up with a sense of "owning" sports. Today's female athletes are committed to letting little girls know that they, too, share that ownership.

All of the WNBA teams take seriously their position as role models. Before games begin, there is a ceremonial ball exchange with young girls from the community. Some teams have kid's clubs and special events for girls at halftime. The Women's Sports Foundation raises money for tickets for girls in WNBA cities to attend games through their "Take a Girl to a Game" program. After games there is time for autograph sessions and opportunities for girls to meet and learn about their teams and players. The audience at WNBA games is always filled with girls (and usually their moms and dads and brothers.)

Kelly Kennedy said her USPV [United States Professional Volleyball] team members always sign autographs and volleyballs after their games. They also visit elementary schools and talk with boys and girls about their sport. Visits like this were never on the agenda when she was in grade school, Kennedy said. She also finds that little boys are just as excited to meet athletic women as the girls are, and high school kids often come over to the elementary schools to see them.

The Chicago Ice also encourages girls to get to know ice hockey. In 1999 they hosted an outing in honor of National Women and Girls in Sports Day, in conjunction with A Sporting Chance Foundation, which encourages girls to participate in sports as a means to develop life skills that lead to self-esteem, responsibility, good body image, and academic achievements. They brought approximately 40 girls to Johnny's Ice House, where the girls visited both the Chicago and St. Louis locker rooms before game time. Players from both teams answered questions and explained the game of hockey to them. The girls cheered and yelled for the Ice during the game, but both teams came away with something more important: the opportunity to meet and interact with some wonderful girls who are the future of women's sports.

Most of the women volleyball players Elaina Oden coaches at Indiana University are there with the help of scholarships, and they get the word out to girls encouraging a love of the sport. Laura Dewitz, 21 said, "We go to Indiana University sporting events together, we hold autograph sessions after games, we volunteer teaching kids to play volleyball [through Hoosier Hitters]."

Across the country hundreds of high school and college women apply for and turn out for WNBA team tryouts whenever they are held. Team managers say they are constantly answering phone inquiries from these young women, too.

Scores of television commercials during broadcasts of women's team games are all about role modeling. The popular WNBA television ads during the 1998 season feature a group of young girls giving some attitude to the players and implying that the younger generation is counting on them. There are also many public service TV ads by companies such as Reebok and Nike that encourage girls to get involved in team sports.

Television commercials heralding the approach of the National Women's Football League, the National Women's Hockey League, and Women's Major League Baseball show young girls in a huddle planning strategy. The theme is, "It's just a matter of time."

9

Lesbianism in Women's Softball Discourages Young Girls from Participating

Kathryn Jean Lopez

Kathryn Jean Lopez is the editor of National Review On-line *and the associate editor of* National Review. *Her award-winning work also appears in a variety of newspapers and magazines. In addition, Lopez is a TV and radio commentator.*

Competitive high school and college softball teams have many lesbian players who often put pressure on their teammates to become involved in lesbian relationships. Straight female athletes frequently feel uncomfortable playing on teams with lesbian athletes because they have to share locker rooms or travel accommodations with them. Many talented softball players have left teams or the sport because they did not like the lesbian domination of the sport.

"On road trips those who were dating roomed with one another and slept together." "Changing in the locker room made me feel very uncomfortable." "The issue was so pervasive at my school that I felt choked out."

That lesbians play softball is a terribly old stereotype, but few outside of college athletics have heard what it's like for a non-gay girl who wants to play the sport. If you're not crazy

Kathryn Jean Lopez, "Leagues of Their Own: The Delicate Question of Lesbians and Softball," *National Review*, vol. 54, October 14, 2002, p. 19. Copyright © 2002 by National Review, Inc., 215 Lexington Ave., New York, NY 10016. Reproduced by permission.

about your daughter showering in a very-far-away-from-don't-ask-don't-tell gym shower, high-school and college softball might not be for her. In *Diamonds Are a Dyke's Best Friend: Reflections, Reminiscences, and Reports from the Field on the Lesbian National Pasttime*, Yvonne Zipter makes a compelling case that softball teams have long been the best way to meet lesbians. She quotes one woman's account: "I'm not saying all women who play softball are gay, but . . . if you think someone is gay and you don't have proof to satisfy your curiosity, [asking 'Have you ever played softball?'] may be a solution."

Of course, when its a recreational softball league for adults, that's no one's business. But it is an issue on high-school and college teams. Zipter cites another experienced player: "I met my first lover through softball. . . . My daughter—she's eighteen—she plays softball. She has a girlfriend, too. They met playing softball in high school together."

Although experiences certainly differ—one coach at a private girls' school, for instance, says lesbian social pressure within softball is waning—the stereotype continues to ring true for many girls today. One woman—now 35—who has played softball since age six and works at a softball-related organization, says that of the hundreds of athletes and coaches she's worked with, "approximately ten" subsequently continued with softball professionally. Many of the women, she says, have independently given her the same reason for throwing in the towel: Oftentimes "not only was there incredible and persistent pressure put on them to participate in and join the lesbian community," but they sometimes were even "pressured to leave."

> **"** It was uncomfortable to dress/undress around those teammates who you knew were gay. **"**

Another girl, from a conservative Catholic family, says she was clueless going into softball. "The older I got the more I began to realize that some of my teammates and close friends were lesbians or bisexual. . . . I noticed that as the competition advanced, the higher the percentage of lesbian players." She wondered, "Was I comfortable enough to be a 'softball player' in a new environment? Did I want that label on me at a new school?" (She eventually quit because of a shoulder injury.)

Still, with the exception of a few small, lesbian publishing houses (e.g., the now-defunct Firebrand Books, publisher of *Diamonds Are a Dyke's Best Friend*), you're not going to find too many people wanting to talk about the issue. In fact, whatever your morality and whatever your lifestyle, hardly anyone wants to touch the topic. As a result, few coaches—especially male coaches—are willing to talk about the L-word, for fear they will be construed as enemies of women's sports. In her book *Strong Women, Deep Closets*, openly lesbian former swimming and basketball coach Pat Griffin complains: "When anyone in women's sport has a grievance or when they want to explain why women's sport is not more popular, lesbians are always a vulnerable and convenient scapegoat."

> ❝ Just a few lesbians on a team can start a trend—whether it be a 'lesbian until graduation' preference, or something more permanent. ❞

So what exactly is the "lesbian problem"? Why can't some girls come out of the closet without straight girls and their parents getting all bent out of shape? As one college-sports insider puts it, "lesbian athletes are often clique-ish within their terms and can be sexually aggressive"—neither of which makes for team spirit. As the same (male) insider puts it: "The fact is that young, athletic college girls are, well, hot. The football players are going to hit on them and, hell, so did I. But their lesbian teammates am hitting on them, too, and what's unique about that is that those teammates share hotel rooms, showers, and locker rooms with them."

In the Locker Room

One college player reports: "It was uncomfortable to dress/undress around those teammates who you knew were gay. It's not that I had the fear that they were pursuing me—that is a line that most don't cross, going after straight people. It's just that I felt the same uncomfortableness that I would feel changing around a guy." Many other straight girls, she says, would never dream of showering with their team. Also, "there was locker-room talk, much like guys do. . . . The girls talk about nasty stuff also." She estimates that in the first team she played for, 50 percent of the team were practicing lesbians, and another 25 percent "were struggling with the issue, riding the fence." This is significant, she says, especially when you consider that female college athletes have "a strict schedule of classes, practices, weights, traveling, etc., and [therefore] little time for guys. As a college softball player you are always around your team." Just a few lesbians on a team can start a trend—whether it be a "lesbian until graduation" preference, or something more permanent.

This woman wound up transferring out of a large state school in order to be able to play softball while avoiding the softball culture. But when she called one particular small Christian college, she didn't get very far. "I told [the coach] my name and the university that I was leaving and explained to him my interest in his school. He cut my sentence off short and said, 'I'm sorry, but we don't need any of your type on our team. We are not that kind of team.' He hung up. He knew the school's rep; he had stereotyped me immediately and didn't even give me a chance to meet him. That hurt."

So what's the solution? Some schools have attempted banning open lesbians from their teams, but that rarely goes over well, at least publicly. Rene Portland, Penn State women's basketball coach, is known for her short-lived "no alcohol, no drugs, no lesbians" rule. The girl who switched schools because of the atmosphere at her first school went on to a smaller school where the married coach consciously tried to recruit so that the usual lesbian cliques could not form. But even there, the girl says, the "team is now [two years later] about one-third gay. You just can't keep it out."

> *At many schools, softball isn't just about wholesome athletic competition.*

One male university athletic official—who, by the way, says he has no moral qualms about homosexuality—suggests a two-part solution. To straights, he says: "Become less homophobic, more tolerant." To gays, he says: "Throwing [gayness] in people's faces doesn't help nurture [tolerance]." But as an administrator, he still faces tough choices. He knows, for example, how to deal with a male coach who gets sexually involved with a female player: You fire him. But with lesbian coaches that's not so easy. "I just wouldn't know what to do," he says, if a lesbian coach were to become involved with a female player. "You've got to walk on eggshells with those issues. . . . People do not want to go there."

But these issues cannot forever remain below the public radar. It may, in fact, be impossible to change softball; but—at the very least—parents and players should know what they are getting into. At many schools, softball isn't just about wholesome athletic competition. To those families who think it is: buyer beware.

10

Too Many Fans Expect Male Athletes to Be Super Masculine

Dennis Rodman

Dennis Rodman played for five championship teams in the National Basketball Association during the 1980s and 1990s. He openly engages in controversial behavior, including wearing women's clothing.

People feel threatened when a male athlete does something that is not considered manly, such as wearing pink or coming out as gay. Male athletes should be able to be gay or bisexual or show their feminine side without having their manhood or status as athletes questioned. People accept that many actors and entertainers are gay and gay athletes should also be able to find the same acceptance when they come out.

"Basketball is a man's sport." "Sports is a man's world." Everybody has an image in their mind of what it means to be an athlete in our society.

I paint my fingernails. I color my hair. I sometimes wear women's clothes.

I want to challenge people's image of what an athlete is supposed to be. I like bringing out the feminine side of Dennis Rodman. I like to shock people, to have them wonder where in the hell I'm coming from. To hang out in a gay bar or put on a sequined halter top makes me feel like a total person and not just a one-dimensional man.

I'm always looking for new ways to test myself, whether it's on the court or off. There are no rules, no boundaries—I'm trying to get deep into who I am. I'm trying to truly discover who I am. I don't think any of us really know who we are, and most people are afraid to let themselves go. They're afraid to take the chance, because they might find out something about themselves they don't really want to know.

Tomorrow I could bring a whole new, totally different dimension to myself. If I want to wear a dress, I'll wear a dress. I'm up for just about anything; I'm still finding my way through the tunnels, looking for that light that gets me into the next version of the state fair.

Immediately, people are going to say: he's gay.

No, that's not what it means. I'm not gay. I would tell you if I was. If I go to a gay bar, that doesn't mean that I want another man to put his tongue down my throat—no. It means I want to be a whole individual. It means I'm comfortable dealing with different people in different situations. It means I'm willing to go out there in the world and see how different people live their lives. There's nothing wrong with that.

> **" I want to challenge people's image of what an athlete is supposed to be. "**

I grew up in a house of women—my mother and two sisters. I thought when I was growing up that I was going to be gay.

I thought that all along, because I had women around me and I wasn't accepted by girls. They thought I was unattractive, and I was so shy around them, it didn't really matter what they thought of me.

That's not to say I repressed my sexuality and now, all of a sudden, I've decided I really want to be gay. I didn't get money and a little bit of power and decide to let the real me loose.

Everything I do is about confidence. After years of struggling with my identity—who I was, who I was going to be—I've become totally confident about being who I am. I can go out to a salon and have my nails painted pink, and then go out and play in the NBA, on national television, with pink nails.

The opinion of other players doesn't make any difference to me. Most of them think I'm insane anyway, so nothing I do now is going to change anything. They look across at me with my painted fingernails and it gives me another psychological edge; now they're looking at me like they really don't know what I'm going to do next.

> *If you look closer, there are so many homosexual aspects of sports.*

I have a pink Harley-Davidson, and I don't care what anybody thinks or says while I'm riding it. My pickup is pink and white. I'm confident enough that I couldn't care less if somebody thinks I'm gay. What I feel inside is this: I know who I am, and there's nothing you can say or think about me that's going to affect me.

It took me a while, but I have the same feeling of confidence and power in my personal life as I have on the basketball court. I took a lot of wrong turns and made a lot of mistakes, but I feel that I'm finally running my own show. Nobody's going to tell me it's not manly to drive a pink truck or wear pink nails. I'll be the judge of my own manliness.

There might be some players in the NBA who are gay. Would that shock people? Probably, but it shouldn't. There might be some players in the league who are bisexual. There are people in any profession who are gay and bisexual, so why should basketball players and athletes be any different? Statistically, it would be almost impossible for the entire sports world to exist without gay or bisexual people.

I'm not pointing the finger at any one guy, because I don't know about other players' personal lives. Also, I don't think it's something you stand around and point fingers about. You don't blame people for this, or ridicule them. If I was gay, I would stand up and say that I am. I would let everyone know that I am gay and existing in what is supposed to be a man's sport.

Homosexual Aspects of Sports

There is so much hypocrisy in sports, bro. Everyone is supposed to be tough and macho. Everyone's a man's man, tough and mean. But if you look closer, there are so many homosexual aspects of sports. It's all swept under the rug, though, because no one wants to admit the reality of things. Everybody says, "No way, that's just teamwork." Sure, we're all part of a team. Everything we do is all in the group, all in the family—man on man.

Just look around. You'd be blind not to see it. Watch any basketball game. Watch any football game. What's the first thing guys do when they win a big game? They hug each other. What does a baseball manager do when he takes his pitcher out? He takes the ball and pats him on the ass. He could shake his hand or punch him on the shoulder, but he doesn't. He pats him directly on the ass. Isiah Thomas and Magic Johnson whispered into each other's ears and kissed each other on the cheek for years before games.

Man hugs man. Man pats man on ass. Man whispers in man's ear and kisses him on the cheek. This is classic homosexual or bisexual behavior. It's in the gay bible. You tell people this and they're like, "Oh, no it's not. It's just a man's thing."

> *It seems that people feel threatened when an athlete does something that is not considered manly.*

And I say, "You're damned right. It *is* a man's thing."

I'm not saying you have to be gay to do these things, but you have to accept that it falls in the large confines of homosexual behavior. You just have to accept that. I do those things on the basketball court—hug a guy, pat a guy on the ass—and if you want to call me homosexual or bisexual because of that, that's fine. I accept that. Then I guess you can take the next step and say I want to sleep with a man. . . .

Being a "Man"

And here's something about the craziness of the sports world that I just don't understand: Whenever a sports figure does something that isn't manly, or if he does something in a way that is not considered manly, everybody gets all upset. It's like, "Oh, God—no way, not *him*."

Why are athletes treated differently than people in everyday society? It seems that people feel threatened when an athlete does something that is not considered manly. It's like they've crossed over some imaginary line that nobody thinks should be crossed.

> *Somehow it's always a scandal when an athlete comes out of the closet.*

Entertainers and actors are not treated the same way. If an entertainer is gay, it's accepted. People accept that without a second thought. But somehow it's always a scandal when an athlete comes out of the closet.

Coming Out

There haven't been that many examples, and I think it's because athletes are afraid of what might happen if they do come out. A baseball player named Glenn Burke had his career ruined because the Dodgers apparently found out he was gay. The team couldn't handle it, they couldn't deal with it. Teams can deal when a guy has a drug problem or an alcohol problem, but not when they find out someone's doing something they don't like in the privacy of their own bedroom. It doesn't make sense.

Maybe when an athlete comes out, people start to wonder: is the world of sports turning into a gay world? I guess athletes are supposed to be completely different from any other walk of life. If a guy who works in your office is gay, it's no big deal. He's just gay. But if a guy who plays basketball or baseball or football comes out and says he's gay, everybody looks at him funny. Nobody can believe it. That doesn't make any sense to me. We're held to a different standard.

People look up to us, and why? I think I have an answer: more than anything else, people play sports and listen to music when they're looking to escape their lives. Or they watch sports and read about sports and talk about sports. So with so many people interested in sports, there's no way it can be accepted if somebody within that community comes out and says he's gay. People trip on that.

This isn't something I can talk to other players about. I can't open up and say, "Have you ever thought about being gay?" There's not a player out there who would say, "Yeah, you know I have. I wish I was gay. I wish I could be." No way a player would ever tell you that, even if it was true.

I'm not trying to encourage kids to be gay, but it shouldn't keep them from being in athletics if they are. You can't say I'm less of a man because I've given some thought to being with another man. I'm not trying to steer kids into saying being gay is cool. You go with your heart, your feelings, and what you desire. Like anything, don't let what other people think decide who you are.

11

Homophobia in Major League Baseball Discourages Gay Teens from Pursuing Baseball Careers

Billy Bean

Billy Bean is a gay male baseball player who played in the major leagues for nine seasons.

Baseball is the American pastime that has always promised equality of opportunity. However, this promise has not been extended to gay players, and Major League Baseball (MLB) has done nothing to help gay players who routinely face harassment and discrimination. As a result, most gay players keep their sexuality a secret and deprive gay teens looking for heroes in the world of team sports. The gay community needs to get involved with the game at every level in order to end discrimination. This involvement includes attaining positions from scout to umpire.

Baseball is a game. But it is also much more—our national pastime, a metaphor for values, a moral undertaking, an international language. It has always reflected, as Nicholas Dawidoff wrote, "the contours of the nation." It's the means by which guys in business suits and guys in construction hats bond over a beer. Gay guys and straight guys can sit elbow to

Billy Bean, with Chris Bull, *Going the Other Way: Lessons from a Life in and out of Major-League Baseball*. New York: Marlowe & Company, 2003. Copyright © 2003 by Billy Bean. Reproduced by permission.

elbow at the sports bar watching the World Series.

But when it comes to gay ballplayers, baseball has not lived up to its promise of equality and opportunity. The greatest game on earth should be leading the way for equality, as it did in the days of racial integration, not lagging behind every other industry in the treatment of gay athletes.

> *When it comes to gay ballplayers, baseball has not lived up to its promise of equality and opportunity.*

I grew up believing the diamond was the fairest, most just place on earth. It was a place where poor kids could get ahead, where white, brown, and black players had an equal chance to succeed, where the scrawny son of a single mother would be judged on performance alone. It was a shock when I realized, in my late twenties after nearly a decade of service, that simply being myself was considered incompatible with pro ball. The malicious, anti-gay climate of the game forced me to make a cruel choice between personal and private life, between love of the game and love of a man.

After all I sacrificed for the game, it pains me that MLB [Major League Baseball] still refuses to take even the most basic steps to help and support its gay players. Harassment and discrimination are allowed to run rampant, forcing many big leaguers to remain closeted. A few straight players have made it known they don't want to share the clubhouse with openly gay teammates. Baseball has allowed the discomfort of these narrow-minded guys to trump the right of gay ballplayers to work in a safe environment.

Because young gay athletes have never seen a role model in male team sports, they assume quite logically that they would be unwelcome in that arena, that the competitive disadvantage would be too great and too unpleasant. They've read the comments of athletes such as Reggie White and John Rocker. They've seen the leagues drag their feet when it comes to improving the atmosphere. Baseball, football, hockey, and basketball offer no hope for gay kids looking for heroes. . . .

Few ballplayers are choirboys off the field, but that doesn't make them bad guys. Unless you play beside them, it's very difficult to know what they are made of. I saw plenty of players lovingly kiss a wife or girlfriend good-bye only to spend the next two weeks on the road screwing around. It was nobody's business but theirs. Yet it seems hypocritical to turn our heads away from heterosexual mischief, while the mere thought of the most committed same-sex companionship is still taboo.

I played with John Wetteland in the Dodger organization for three years. He was a hell-raiser with one of the best heaters around, one of those zany characters right out of *Bull Durham*. He drove other players nuts with his practical jokes. Since he was a blue-chip prospect, he could get away with just about anything. I'll never forget the night he came bounding into the hotel room I was sharing with Dave Hansen in Albuquerque. A bunch of us were seated around a table playing cards. He proudly showed off what other players termed his "brown trout hall of fame," an album of photographs he'd taken the previous season of his, and some of his teammates', most impressive contributions to the Texas sewer system while he was playing in San Antonio.

So imagine my surprise when I picked up the July 27, 1997, edition of *The New York Times Magazine* to find a big photo of Wetteland in the locker room. "How Can A Moral Wrong Be A Civil Right?" read the T-shirt he was wearing, a disparaging reference to gay-rights causes. John had become a born-again Christian. "Jesus Christ is my point man," he said.

> *Wouldn't it be more productive for Major League Baseball and its thirty clubs to include sexual orientation in its anti-discrimination clause?*

I'm happy John found religion. I'm a spiritual person myself. The world is full of beauty, and I believe that we were all created for a reason. But John is a classic case of a ballplayer who forgets where he came from and what got him to the top. The idea that Jesus would have scorned equality is an antiquated manipulation of scripture. As far as I'm concerned, the ultra-right-wing Fellowship of Christian Athletes, which has campaigned against gays and never asks athletes to take a hard look at their own values, deserves a place in Wetteland's old photo album.

I admired Will Clark for his comment in that same article. "Hey, I congratulate you on doing something for your life," the sweet-swinging lefty told a teammate who gave up a home run and attributed it to God's will. "But this is about baseball. And you'd better go out there and do it yourself. The Lord didn't hang that slider."

The MLB Must Condemn Harassment

John Rocker is a left-handed relief pitcher with nasty stuff. He zoomed to fame with his unpredictable 97-miles-per-hour fastball, showing his stuff on national television during the National League play-offs three years in a row when he played for the Atlanta Braves.

Rocker also has some nasty attitudes. In 2001, he told *Sports Illustrated* that minority groups were despicable, complaining about "all the queers with AIDS who ride the 7 train in New York City." America is a free country, and John Rocker has a right to speak his mind. But it's just plain wrong for ballplayers to encourage prejudice, and Rocker has paid a heavy price for his venomous words—he was fined, suspended, and banished to the minors. Many people called him an idiot. They may be right.

At the same time, he simply got caught saying what some people think but are afraid to say. Ballplayers, worried about their reputations, have learned to spout politically correct lines fed by agents and handlers.

> *It's asking a lot for a ballplayer, having devoted his life to the game, to shoulder the burden for a cause, no matter how worthy.*

It's easier for baseball to blame the outburst on the player than look in the mirror. Wouldn't it be more productive for Major League Baseball and its thirty clubs to include sexual orientation in its anti-discrimination clause? I'd rather MLB do what virtually every other industry does today: institute more aggressive diversity-awareness training that includes sexual orientation. They need to make it clear that harassment won't be allowed on the field or in the locker room. As it now stands, a case could be made that all thirty big-league clubs and dozens more minor-league ones are in violation of Title VII of the Civil Rights Act.

The Major League Baseball Players Association, of which I'm a member, should make the case for sexual orientation non-discrimination, as other unions routinely do. As the association has made clear, baseball is a workplace, not a playground. In states and municipalities with gay-rights laws on the books, baseball clubs may actually be violating anti-discrimination statutes by allowing a hostile workplace.

John Rocker and I could have coexisted on the same team. I played long enough to know that a baseball clubhouse is one of the most diverse places on earth. There are as many prejudices as there are players. Most of the differences have nothing to do with race, religion, or even sexuality. As Doug Brocail put it so well, it's all about character—whether a guy's a team player, whether he plays through injuries, whether he comes to play every day. Everything else is irrelevant. Baseball must make it so.

"I'm Not Gay"

Baseball touts itself as a game without borders, when in fact it is filled with obstacles both obvious and invisible. There are plenty of players locked in the baseball closet. During my playing days, there were always guys I got the "vibe" from, some of whom were among the game's greatest players. With more than 750 big leaguers at any one time, it's not difficult to imagine a dozen or so gay ballplayers.

In the summer of 2002, Mets manager Bobby Valentine told *Details* magazine that the big leagues are "probably ready for an openly gay player. . . . The players are a diverse enough group now that I think they could handle" a gay teammate. The media took this to mean that Valentine was clearing the way for one of his own players to come out. They zeroed in on Mike Piazza, the team's slugging catcher. No evidence was offered for this rumor.

Over a decade ago, Mike and I played together in the Dodger organization. We got to know each other in part because we shared the same agent, Dennis Gilbert. I enjoyed watching him go from a sixty-second-round draft pick to a sure first-ballot Hall of Famer. The guy can rake.

Overall, I thought Mike handled the rumors like the pro he is. Yet I was disappointed with his response to questions about his sexual orientation. "I'm not gay. I'm heterosexual," he declared. Then he added, "In this day and age it would be irrelevant. If the guy is doing his job on the field . . . I don't think there would be any problem at all."

Aside from the redundancy in that first part of his statement, Piazza missed an opportunity to send a message. He could have refused to answer or asked, "Why does it matter?" Once again, young gays and lesbians were reminded how important it is for a superstar to be outspokenly straight, whether he actually is or not. Even so, it was nice to hear that one of the game's best and most respected players wouldn't have a problem with a gay teammate.

> *My own experience shows that the game can indeed handle a qualified gay person in a prominent position.*

Shortly after this episode, I started getting interview requests to talk about Valentine and Piazza, which I did. The informative Web site Outsports.com criticized me for speaking about the career-threatening dangers of coming out publicly at the major-league level, saying that I was encouraging players to stay closeted. I even made a guest appearance on a July 2002 episode of the HBO series *Arli$$* built around this premise. (Dennis Gilbert was the inspiration for the Arliss Michaels character, which was created by Robert Wuhl. Doing the show was like going back in time, only now everything was better. I actually got to act out the kind of supportive, sensible conversations about being a gay ballplayer I wished I could've had with Dennis.)

It's asking a lot for a ballplayer, having devoted his life to the game, to shoulder the burden for a cause, no matter how worthy. The stakes are extraordinarily high. Who protects him—or her—from bigoted fans? And from the manager, or the free-rein front office? All you have to do is look at what happened to Glenn Burke.[1] Times have changed, sure. But how much?

The speculation about who will become the first active player to openly identify as gay remains a hot topic for sports talk radio. Until that happens, MLB is off the hook; it doesn't

---

1. Glenn Burke was a talented outfielder who was driven out of baseball for being openly gay.

have to bother with creating the conditions that would make it possible for gay players to be themselves.

After I came out, commissioner Bud Selig received complaints from fans upset about the prejudice I described in the game. In an August 2000 letter to Outsports.com, Selig responded, "Everyone who wants an opportunity in Major League Baseball, and is deserving of that opportunity, should have that chance."

To me, this sounds like boilerplate. In the 2002 labor negotiations, ownership won major concessions from the formidable players union and Selig stared down [New York Yankees team owner] George Steinbrenner. But when it comes to making the locker room and the diamond safe for gay players, he ducks and heads for cover.

The Gay Community Needs to Get Involved

The responsibility should not fall to MLB alone. The gay and lesbian community must also share the burden for integrating baseball, and it's not enough to scream discrimination from ballpark parking lots. We need to get involved in the game on every level. If the teams themselves aren't mature enough to handle a gay player yet, there are plenty of other places to start. There still isn't a single openly gay scout, front-office exec, coach, or even umpire.

My own experience shows that the game can indeed handle a qualified gay person in a prominent position. There are plenty of baseball people, both on the field and off, who can be relied on in this mission. Shortly after *The New York Times* article appeared in 1999, I received a call on my cell phone. I was surprised to hear from John McHale, Jr., who at the time was the chief executive officer of the Detroit Tigers.

"Billy, I just want you to know that you were once and will always be a member of the Tigers," he said. "You have my support and the support of this organization. Once you wear the Old English *D* on your chest, it can never be taken away."

McHale, who went on to take a similar post with the Tampa Bay Devil Rays, invited me to be his guest at the next opening day at Tiger Stadium. I wasn't able to take him up on his offer, but it meant a lot to hear from this respected baseball man on the team I broke in with. Once again, the message was clear. The loyalty of a team supersedes almost everything that divides human beings.

Organizations to Contact

The editors have compiled the following list of organizations concerned with the issues debated in this book. The descriptions are derived from materials provided by the organizations. All have publications or information available for interested readers. The list was compiled on the date of publication of the present volume; names, addresses, phone and fax numbers, and e-mail addresses may change. Be aware that many organizations take several weeks or longer to respond to inquiries, so allow as much time as possible.

America's Athletes with Disabilities
National Headquarters
8630 Fenton St., Suite 920, Silver Spring, MD 20910
(800) 238-7632 • fax: (301) 589-9052
Web site: www.americasathletes.org

America's Athletes with Disabilities sponsors athletic events for youths and adults with disabilities.

Athletes for Education Foundation (AFE)
PO Box 900517, San Diego, CA 92190
(619) 583-4955 • fax: (619) 287-0358
e-mail: afe85@cox.net • Web site: www.afefoundation.org

The Athletes for Education Foundation is a nonprofit organization of professional athletes, entertainers, and business and community leaders who raise funds to benefit youth programs that promote health and emotional wellness. AFE also provides a mentorship and scholarship program.

Center for the Study of Sport in Society
Northeastern University
360 Huntington Ave., Suite 161 CP, Boston, MA 02115
(617) 373-4025 • fax: (617) 373-4566
Web site: www.sportinsociety.org

The center's mission is to increase awareness of sport and its relation to society and to develop programs that identify problems, offer solutions, and promote the benefits of sport. Its publications include the annual *Racial Report Card.*

Champions in Life Program
U.S. Olympic Training Center, National Headquarters
One Olympic Plaza, Colorado Springs, CO 80909
(719) 866-4500
Web site: www.usoc.org

Champions in Life is an outreach program of the U.S. Olympic Committee that seeks to shape the lives of young people. Olympic and paralympic athletes in the program speak to students about topics such as staying in school, staying drug free, and avoiding gangs and violence. Athletes also conduct demonstrations on a variety of Olympic sports.

Citizenship Through Sports Alliance (CTSA)
23550 W. 105th St., Olathe, KS 66051-1325
(913) 791-9564 • fax: (913) 791-9555
e-mail: jleavens@sportsmanship.org
Web site: www.sportsmanship.org

The Citizenship Through Sports Alliance is a coalition of professional and amateur athletics organizations focused on character in sport and promoting fair play at all levels. CTSA initiatives include the annual Citizenship Through Sports Awards and the Stay in Bounds character education programs.

Gay & Lesbian Athletics Foundation, Inc. (GLAF)
PO Box 425034, Cambridge, MA 02142
(617) 588-0600 • fax: (617) 588-0600
e-mail: info@glaf.org • Web site: www.glaf.org

The Gay & Lesbian Athletics Foundation seeks to create a community of gay athletes who can communicate with each other regularly and help cultivate an environment in sports in which athletes are accepted and respected without regard to their sexual orientation. GLAF hopes that in the process of meeting the first two goals, it can create positive gay athletic role models for the society at large.

National Alliance for Youth Sports
2050 Vista Pkwy., West Palm Beach, FL 33411
(800) 729-2057 • fax: (561) 684-2546
e-mail: nays@nays.org • Web site: www.nays.org

The National Alliance for Youth Sports is a nonprofit organization that works to provide safe, fun, and positive sports for America's youth. It provides certification programs for coaches, officials, and administrators and participates in programs to prevent child abuse and encourage parental involvement in youth sports. The alliance operates the National Clearinghouse for Youth Sports Information, which provides access to many publications and instructional materials pertaining to youth sports.

National Collegiate Athletic Association (NCAA)
6201 College Blvd., Overland Park, KS 66211-2422
(913) 339-1906
Web site: www.ncaa.org

The NCAA is the administrative body overseeing intercollegiate athletic programs. It publishes reports on student-athlete graduation rates in colleges, transcripts from its annual conventions discussing academic and athletic rules, and special reports on sports programs, finances, and television. Among its publications are *NCAA: The Voice of College Sports* and the *Guide for the College-Bound Student-Athlete.*

Native American Sports Council (NASC)
1235 Lake Plaza Dr., Suite 221, Colorado Springs, CO 80906
(719) 632-5282 • fax: (719) 632-5614
Web site: www.nascsports.org

The Native American Sports Council's mission is to promote athletic excellence and wellness within Native American communities through sports programs that combine traditional Native American values with those of the modern Olympics. In cooperation with the U.S. Olympic Committee, NASC offers sport and athlete development programs that enable emerging elite athletes to be identified and developed for national, international, and Olympic competition.

Women's Sports Foundation
Eisenhower Park, East Meadow, NY 11554
(516) 542-4700 • (800) 227-3988 • fax: (516) 542-4716
e-mail: WoSport@aol.com
Web site: www.womenssportsfoundation.org

The foundation supports the participation of women in sports and seeks to educate the public about athletic opportunities for women. It publishes a quarterly newsletter, *The Woman's Sports Experience;* books, including *Aspire Higher—Careers in Sports for Women* and *A Woman's Guide to Coaching;* as well as an annual *College Scholarship Guide.*

World Anti-Doping Agency (WADA)
Stock Exchange Tower
800 Place Victoria, Suite 1700, Montreal, QC H4Z 1B7 Canada
(514) 904-9232 • fax: (514) 904-8650
e-mail: info@wada-ama.org
Web site: www.wada-ama.org

The World Anti-Doping Agency was created in 1999 through a collective initiative led by the International Olympic Committee. The goal of WADA is eradicating the improper use of drugs in sport and creating a level playing field for all athletes.

Bibliography

Books

Ira Berkow	*The Minority Quarterback, and Other Lives in Sports.* Chicago: Ivan R. Dee, 2002.
Larry Bird	*Birdwatching: On Playing and Coaching the Game I Love.* New York: Warner, 1999.
Kim Doren and Charlie Jones	*You Go Girl: Winning the Woman's Way.* Kansas City, MO: Andrews McMeel, 2000.
Stephen J. Dubner	*Confessions of a Hero Worshiper.* New York: William Morrow, 2003.
John R. Gerdy	*Sports: The All-American Addiction.* Jackson: University Press of Mississippi, 2002.
Stephen Jay Gould	*Triumph and Tragedy in Mudville: A Lifelong Passion for Baseball.* New York: W.W. Norton, 2003.
Richard E. Lapchick	*Smashing Barriers: Race and Sport in the New Millennium.* Lanham, MD: Madison, 2001.
Tara Magdalinski and Timothy J.L. Chandler, eds.	*With God on Their Side: Sport in the Service of Religion.* New York: Routledge, 2002.
Randy Martin and Toby Miller, eds.	*SportCult.* Minneapolis: University of Minnesota Press, 1999.
Toby Miller	*Sportsex.* Philadelphia: Temple University Press, 2001.
Jim Reisler, ed.	*Voices of the Oral Deaf: Fourteen Role Models Speak Out.* Jefferson, NC: McFarland, 2002.
Laura Robinson	*Black Tights: Women, Sport, and Sexuality.* Toronto: HarperCollins, 2002.
Sharon Robinson	*Jackie's Nine: Jackie Robinson's Values to Live By.* New York: Scholastic, 2001.
Mark S. Rosentraub	*Major League Losers: The Real Cost of Sports and Who's Paying for It.* New York: Basic Books, 1999.
Curt Sampson	*Chasing Tiger.* New York: Atria, 2002.
Joli Sandoz and Joby Winans, eds.	*Whatever It Takes: Women on Women's Sport.* New York: Farrar, Straus and Giroux, 1999.
Christopher M. Spence	*The Skin I'm In: Racism, Sports, and Education.* Halifax, Canada: Fernwood, 2000.

Murray Sperber   *Beer and Circus: How Big-Time College Sports Is Crip-
                        pling Undergraduate Education.* New York: Henry
                        Holt, 2000.

Daniel L. Wann et al.   *Sports Fans: The Psychology and Social Impact of Spec-
                        tators.* New York: Routledge, 2001.

Andrew Zimbalist   *Unpaid Professionals: Commercialism and Conflict in
                        Big-Time College Sports.* Princeton, NJ: Princeton
                        University Press, 1999.

Periodicals

Harvey Araton   "The Temptations of Success," *New York Times*,
                        April 4, 2004.

Susan Beck   "The Straight Dope," *American Lawyer*, October
                        2001.

David Bjerklie   "How Doctors Help the Dopers: New Ideas from
and Alice Park   Medical Research Are Being Plundered by Athletes
                        Looking for a Boost," *Time*, August 16, 2004.

Kelly Candaele   "Where Are the Jocks for Justice? Cultural Changes
and Peter Dreier   and Lucrative Endorsements May Explain a Drop
                        in Activism," *Nation*, June 28, 2004.

Michael J. Diacin,   "Voices of Male Athletes on Drug Use, Drug
Janet B. Parks, and   Testing, and the Existing Order in Intercollegiate
Pamela C. Allison   Athletics," *Journal of Sport Behavior*, March 2003.

Marilyn Cram   "Athletes as Role Models: Looking for a Good Role
Donahue   Model? Here's What You Need to Know," *Current
                        Health 2*, January 2002.

Joseph Epstein   "Bats, Balls, and Idols," *American Enterprise*, Sep-
                        tember 2000.

Darcy Frey   "Betrayed by the Game," *New York Times Magazine*,
                        February 15, 2004.

Jenna Fryer   "Panthers Move Past Sordid Side, into Super
                        Bowl," Associated Press, January 24, 2004.

William Norman   "Strength from Above," *New American*, September
Grigg   10, 2001.

Michael Henderson   "Pique Practice," *Spectator*, July 20, 2002.

Michael Lewis   "Coach Fitz's Management Theory," *New York
                        Times Magazine*, March 28, 2004.

Mike Lopresti   "Athletes and Politicians Alike Fall Short as Role
                        Models," *Olympian*, January 22, 2004.

Thom Loverro   "Iverson's All Right with Kids," *Washington Times*,
                        July 16, 2002.

Gordon Monson   "Misplaced Role Models Disappoint," *Salt Lake Tri-
                        bune*, July 20, 2003.

Thad Mumford — "The New Minstrel Show: Black Vaudeville with Statistics," *New York Times*, May 23, 2004.

David C. Ogden and Michael L. Hilt — "Collective Identity and Basketball: An Explanation for the Decreasing Number of African-Americans on America's Baseball Diamonds," *Journal of Leisure Research*, vol. 35, 2003.

Richard Roeper — "Patriotism Has Long Been an Olympic Event," *Chicago Sun-Times*, May 19, 2004.

Michael Sokolove — "The Lab Animal," *New York Times Magazine*, January 18, 2004.

Brent Staples — "Broken Hoop Dreams for the Basketball Players of Coney Island," *New York Times*, February 1, 2004.

Mark Starr — "Blowing the Whistle on Drugs: A Raid on a California Laboratory Threatens to Blemish American Athletes—Again," *Newsweek*, November 3, 2003.

Robert Sullivan — "Big Bucks and Baseball: The Idea of Overpaying for an Athlete's Services Didn't Start with A-Rod and It Won't End with Him," *Time*, December 25, 2000.

Taki Theodoracopulos — "Do It My Way," *Spectator*, March 2, 2002.

Anthony Wilson-Smith — "The Unsporting Life: In Which We See Why Pro Athletes Aren't to Blame," *Maclean's*, February 17, 2003.

Index